New Directions for Adult and Continuing Education

Susan Imel
Jovita M. Ross-Gordon
COEDITORS-IN-CHIEF

Bodies of Knowledge: Embodied Learning in Adult Education

Randee Lipson Lawrence
EDITOR

Number 134 • Summer 2012
Jossey-Bass
San Francisco

BODIES OF KNOWLEDGE: EMBODIED LEARNING IN ADULT EDUCATION
Randee Lipson Lawrence (ed.)
New Directions for Adult and Continuing Education, no. 134
Susan Imel, Jovita M. Ross-Gordon, Coeditors-in-Chief

© 2012 Wiley Periodicals, Inc., A Wiley Company. All rights reserved. No part of this publication may be reproduced, stored in a retrieval system, or transmitted in any form or by any means, electronic, mechanical, photocopying, recording, scanning, or otherwise, except as permitted under Section 107 or 108 of the 1976 United States Copyright Act, without either the prior written permission of the publisher or authorization through payment of the appropriate per-copy fee to the Copyright Clearance Center, 222 Rosewood Drive, Danvers, MA 01923; (978) 750-8400, fax (978) 646-8600. The copyright notice appearing at the bottom of the first page of an article in this journal indicates the copyright holder's consent that copies may be made for personal or internal use, or for personal or internal use of specific clients, on the condition that the copier pay for copying beyond that permitted by law. This consent does not extend to other kinds of copying, such as copying for distribution, for advertising or promotional purposes, for creating collective works, or for resale. Such permission requests and other permission inquiries should be addressed to the Permissions Department, c/o John Wiley & Sons, Inc., 111 River Street, Hoboken, NJ 07030; (201) 748-6011, fax (201) 748-6008, www.wiley.com/go/permissions.

Microfilm copies of issues and articles are available in 16mm and 35mm, as well as microfiche in 105mm, through University Microfilms Inc., 300 North Zeeb Road, Ann Arbor, Michigan 48106-1346.

NEW DIRECTIONS FOR ADULT AND CONTINUING EDUCATION (ISSN 1052-2891, electronic ISSN 1536-0717) is part of The Jossey-Bass Higher and Adult Education Series and is published quarterly by Wiley Subscription Services, Inc., A Wiley Company, at Jossey-Bass, One Montgomery Street, Suite 1200, San Francisco, CA 94104-4594. Periodicals Postage Paid at San Francisco, California, and at additional mailing offices. POSTMASTER: Send address changes to New Directions for Adult and Continuing Education, Jossey-Bass, One Montgomery Street, Suite 1200, San Francisco, CA 94104-4594.

New Directions for Adult and Continuing Education is indexed in CIJE: Current Index to Journals in Education (ERIC); Contents Pages in Education (T&F); ERIC Database (Education Resources Information Center); Higher Education Abstracts (Claremont Graduate University); and Sociological Abstracts (CSA/CIG).

SUBSCRIPTIONS for print and electronic in the U.S. cost $98.00 for individuals and $316.00 for institutions, agencies, and libraries.

EDITORIAL CORRESPONDENCE should be sent to the Coeditors-in-Chief, Susan Imel, ERIC/ACVE, 1900 Kenny Road, Columbus, Ohio 43210-1090, e-mail: imel.1@osu.edu; or Jovita M. Ross-Gordon, Southwest Texas State University, EAPS Dept., 601 University Drive, San Marcos, TX 78666.

Cover photograph by Jack Hollingsworth@Photodisc

www.josseybass.com

Contents

EDITOR'S NOTES 1
Randee Lipson Lawrence

1. Intuitive Knowing and Embodied Consciousness 5
Randee Lipson Lawrence
This article describes the relationship between intuition and embodied knowing, including how embodied knowing comes into our consciousness. It sets the stage for the variety of practice contexts and strategies that are discussed in this volume.

2. Embodied Learning and Patient Education: From Nurses' Self-Awareness to Patient Self-Caring 15
Ann L. Swartz
This article presents embodied learning from a neurobiologic perspective as a naturally occurring process in patient education. It describes how nursing students learned to trust their own bodies, which led to self-empowerment and extended to patient care.

3. Embodied Learning at Work: Making the Mind-set Shift from Workplace to Playspace 25
Pamela Meyer
Creative play and improvisation can transform organizations into dynamic spaces for learning, promoting collaboration, and creating problem solving.

4. Embodying Women's Stories for Community Awareness and Social Action 33
Yolanda Nieves
This article describes a case study involving collecting stories of Puerto Rican women and embodying them through community performance. In performing the stories, repressed and subjugated knowledge was unleashed.

5. Outdoor Experiential Education: Learning Through the Body 43
Eric Howden
In adventure education, one experiences a series of physical challenges designed to improve self-confidence and create cohesive teams. As thinking one's way through the obstacles often promotes anxiety, one learns to rely on one's body.

6. Dance as a Way of Knowing 53
Celeste Snowber
Dance is a method of inquiry that invites us to imagine new worlds. This article takes an in-depth look at dance and body movement and the implications for teaching and learning in a variety of disciplines.

7. Embodied Knowledge and Decolonization: Walking with 61
Theater's Powerful and Risky Pedagogy
Shauna Butterwick, Jan Selman
Popular theater is an educational tool that empowers individuals to see themselves as creators of their own stories. Mind, body, and emotions come together as anti-oppressive forces.

8. Coming Full Circle: Reclaiming the Body 71
Randee Lipson Lawrence
This concluding article integrates and synthesizes themes from the previous articles and highlights the lessons learned.

Index 79

Editor's Notes

Everyone has a body. This is a known fact. While we don't all speak the same verbal language, the universal language of the body is something that all human beings share. The body has wisdom and knowledge of its own.

Embodied or somatic learning is a way of learning that relies on the body's knowledge. Our most basic form of learning in childhood is preverbal; however, traditional schooling forces us to check our bodies at the door, requiring us to sit at a desk and raise our hands, focusing primarily on cognition to the exclusion of other ways of knowing. By the time we reach adulthood, "being in our bodies" is a foreign concept and a source of discomfort for many of us.

This volume challenges the dominant paradigm of how knowledge is constructed and shared. When Rene Descartes in the seventeenth century proclaimed "I think therefore I am," he started a movement privileging the mind as the sole source of human dialogue (Miller, 2007). This volume contests the Cartesian dualistic belief of the mind being separate from the body by calling attention to the body as a source of learning.

Embodied learning, while beginning to gain attention in adult education literature (see Merriam, Caffarella, and Baumgartner, 2007; Boucouvalas and Lawrence, 2010), is the least discussed method of learning. Previous volumes of *New Directions for Adult and Continuing Education* have focused on spiritual knowing (English and Gillen, 2000) and affective knowing (Dirkx, 2008). This volume complements those previous publications by exploring the multiple ways adults learn through their bodies.

This volume views embodied learning through a variety of practice contexts, including higher education, community education, health care, and the workplace, and through multiple methods, including dance, theater, and outdoor experiential education.

In Chapter One, I explore embodied knowing as an intuitive process. I begin with a discussion of how embodied knowing comes into our conscious awareness and introduce a model of intuitive knowing that situates the body as the foundation for other interconnected ways of knowing. I then discuss how to access and use embodied knowing in practice.

Chapter Two focuses on embodied knowing in the health care professions, particularly as it relates to patient education. Ann L. Swartz offers stories from her own experience as well as those of her patients and nursing students to illustrate how, when people learn to listen and connect more deeply to their body, they can be guided to what the body needs to get healthy.

In Chapter Three, Pamela Meyer describes how workplaces can be transformed into playspaces. She describes a case study of an organization where embodied practices are a way of life. These practices improve relationships among the workers, generate high energy and engagement, and facilitate collaboration that extends into the workday. Meyer offers suggestions for facilitators to engage in playful embodied learning.

Yolanda Nieves shares a community awareness project in Chapter Four. In a Puerto Rican community in Chicago, she created an ensemble theater piece that embodied the stories of women's subjugated knowledge. The performance was created as an adult education tool to promote awareness and social action.

Outdoor adventure education is introduced in Chapter Five. Eric Howden discusses this form of experiential education, where mind-body connections are made explicit. Participants are faced with an increasingly challenging set of experiences that bring the body and mind into direct conflict. Powerful learning occurs as these conflicts are resolved.

Chapter Six focuses on dance as a method of inquiry. Celeste Snowber explains how the embodied nature of dance reconnects us to our true selves. Snowber connects dance to literacy, critical thinking, and other learning processes. Dance is a way of grappling with and making sense of a complex world.

In Chapter Seven, Shauna Butterwick and Jan Selman discuss popular theater as a powerful tool for disrupting forces that colonize and oppress. They offer examples from their practice of how participants can use theater to embody their stories and emphasize creating a safe and respectful environment.

Chapter Eight provides a summary and synthesis of the major themes in the previous articles, emphasizing ways to reclaim the body as a source of knowledge.

The contributors to this volume are in a sense pioneers. They have dared to espouse a way of knowing that has been all but absent in adult and higher education. Perhaps the lack of embodied practice is because educators are still steeped in "epistemologies of ignorance" (Malewski and Jaramillo, 2011), meaning a blind adherence to the canon or dominant discourses in education. Perhaps they are fearful of the body, or perhaps they just have not been exposed to other ways of knowing. It is our hope through this volume that educators in all contexts will reconsider what is means to know, what body wisdom has to teach us, and how embodied learning can help learners to fulfill their human potential.

Randee Lipson Lawrence
Editor

References

Boucouvalas, M., and Lawrence, R. L. "Adult Learning." In C. E. Kasworm, A. D. Rose, and J. M. Ross-Gordon (eds.), *Handbook of Adult and Continuing Education*. Los Angeles: Sage, 2010.

Dirkx, J. (ed.). *Adult Learning and the Emotional Self*. New Directions for Adult and Continuing Education, no.120. San Francisco: Jossey-Bass, 2008.
English, L. M., and Gillen, M. A. (eds.). *Addressing the Spiritual Needs of Adult Learning: What Educators Can Do*. New Directions for Adult and Continuing Education, no. 85. San Francisco: Jossey-Bass, 2000.
Malewski, E., and Jaramillo, N. (eds.). *Epistemologies of Ignorance in Education*. Charlotte, N.C.: Information Age, 2011.
Merriam, S., Caffarella, R., and Baumgartner, L. *Learning in Adulthood*. San Francisco: Jossey-Bass, 2007.
Miller, J. P. *The Holistic Curriculum*. Toronto, Canada: University of Toronto Press, 2007.

RANDEE LIPSON LAWRENCE *is an associate professor of adult and continuing education at National Louis University in Chicago.*

This article explores the role of intuition as a preconscious embodied state and its implication for adult education.

Intuitive Knowing and Embodied Consciousness

Randee Lipson Lawrence

Imagine you are walking down a dimly lit street in an unfamiliar neighborhood. It is just before sunset and the streets are fairly deserted. Suddenly you hear a loud noise that might be a car backfiring, or it might even be gunshots. Your heart starts racing, your breathing becomes shallow, and you feel as if you may start to hyperventilate. Some instinct tells you to run and leave the area as quickly as possible. You don't stop to think or reason or figure out what is happening, you just follow your body's cues and move toward safety. You rely on your intuition.

Intuition

Intuitive knowing is one of the most complex and misunderstood ways of knowing. It is difficult to put into words and verbalize. Intuition has been defined as "the ability to perceive or know things without conscious reasoning" (Webster's New World College Dictionary); "a way of knowing that transcends intellect and reason" (Vaughan, 1979, p. 111); and "a realization of wholeness which is simultaneously internal and external, it is an event which is both experiential and cognitive" (Blanchard, 1993, p. 10). According to Jung (1964), intuition is one of two ways to gain access to certain experiences or events that are not part of our conscious awareness.

Intuition is spontaneous, heart-centered, free, adventurous, imaginative, playful, nonsequential, and nonlinear (Lawrence, 2009). We access intuitive knowledge through dreams, symbols, artwork, dance, yoga, meditation, contemplation, and immersion in nature. Most of these processes call upon embodied knowing. This chapter examines embodied knowing as an intuitive process and discusses how embodied knowledge comes into our conscious awareness, how embodied knowing is connected to other ways of knowing, and how educators can incorporate an embodied pedagogy into their practice.

Embodied Learning by Any Other Name

In addition to the word *embodied*, there are other terms that relate to learning through the body. In his well-known taxonomy, Bloom (1956/1984) discussed the psychomotor domain of learning, which he differentiated from the cognitive and affective domains. Learning in the psychomotor domain includes using one's body to perform tasks or engaging in physical activity such as throwing a ball or constructing a building. Gardner (1993) talked about bodily-kinesthetic intelligence as one of the nine multiple intelligences that human beings possess. According to Gardner, we all have one or more dominant intelligence areas. Bodily-kinesthetic intelligence involves learning by doing, as in building and making things, muscle movement, dancing, and athletics. It is the preferred mode of many surgeons, builders, and others who work with their hands. Kinesthetic learners prefer to take a hands-on approach to learning as opposed to hearing a lecture or observing.

In a critique of Gardner, Parviainen (2010) argued that bodily-kinesthetic intelligence cannot be separated from spatial intelligence. Dancers and other performers need to perceive and interact with the spaces and others around them, so movement cannot be looked at in isolation.

Freiler (2008) defined somatic learning as "learning directly experienced through bodily awareness and sensation during purposive body-centered movements" (p. 39). Her research participants spoke about "'being in tune' to or with their bodies, 'listening to' the body as it talks to them and tells them something and 'being more aware' of attending to body experiences and one's surroundings." Similarly, Stuckey (2009) defined body/somatic knowledge as "learning that comes from the body through engagement with the senses and an increased bodily awareness" (p. 33). Although some writers distinguish between these terms, this chapter uses the term *embodied knowing* with the understanding that it also encompasses these other terms.

Integrated Ways of Knowing

I have been interested in holistic knowing or knowledge at the intersections of body, mind, heart, and spirit and their relationship to intuition for the past decade (see Lawrence, 2008, 2009; Lawrence and Dirkx, 2010). I have developed a working model to help explain these ways of knowing (see Figure 1). The model shows an upside down triangle.

Figure 1. Intuitive Holistic Knowing.

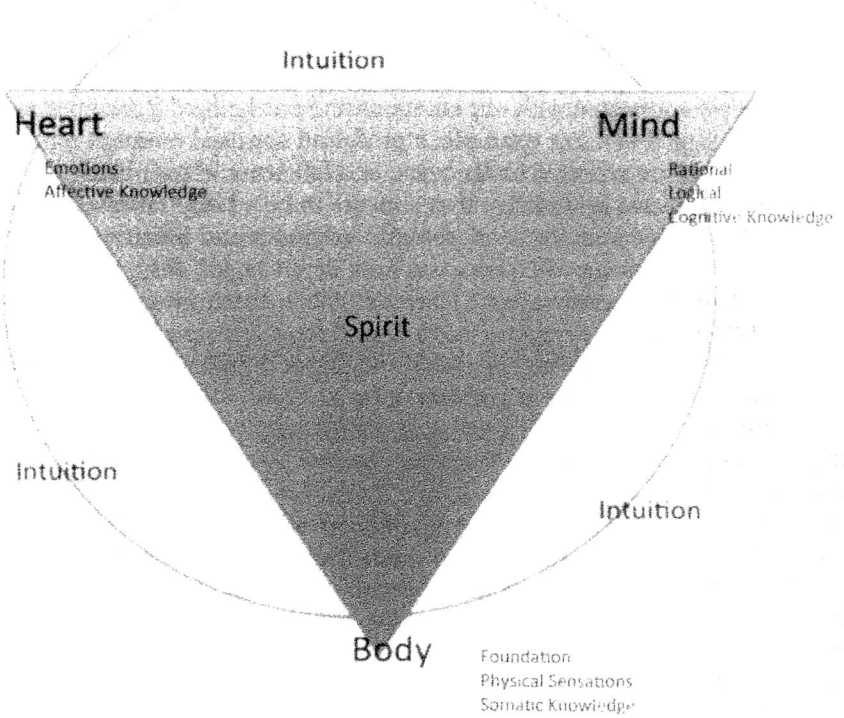

Heart (affective knowledge) and mind (cognitive knowledge) are at the two points at the top of the triangle. The body is at the bottom, and spiritual knowledge is "grayed out" in the center, as it is difficult to grasp but is at the center of all knowledge. Embodied knowing is at the bottom because it is foundational. The most primal way of accessing knowledge is through the body as our earliest forms of knowing are preverbal. Babies know in their bodies when they are experiencing distress or discomfort months or years before they learn the words for these feelings. As babies become toddlers, they explore their world first through touch. While they may hear a parent's warning not to go near the cactus plant because it can be dangerous, it is not until they experience the prickly sensation directly that they learn to stay away.

Knowledge is present in the body before it reaches our conscious awareness. For example, tension is first experienced in the body as a stiff neck, queasy stomach, or tight jaw. If we examine the sources of this disease, we may be able to trace it to a particular experience or event.

Many of our strong emotions include a physical component. When we are sad or depressed, we feel a heaviness that is palpable. Fear may be experienced by a quickening of the heart rate or hyperventilation. As Parviainen (2010) pointed out, the words *motion* and *emotion* have the same root. When we have strong emotional reactions, we describe the experience as *being moved*.

The spiritual domain "reflects a sense of the sacred, mystery or awe, and is deeply connected with our emotions and our bodies" (Lawrence and Dirkx, 2010, p. 149). For example, a profound spiritual moment may be experienced by unexpected chills, tears, or a felt sense of well-being.

Even cognitive knowledge that appears to be wholly rational on the surface often has affective and somatic components. Mezirow (2000) described disorienting dilemmas, such as death or job loss, that create opportunities for transformative learning. While Mezirow suggested that reflective discourse is the way to move toward transformative learning, these dilemmas always come with emotional and physical dimensions that beg to be resolved at least in part in embodied ways.

Consciousness

Although we can talk about these ways of knowing as separate domains, they are very much interconnected and intuitive. Intuitive knowledge exists even before it comes into our conscious awareness. As mentioned, we first experience this knowledge in our body. Crowdes (2000, p. 27) used the term *conscious embodiment*, which "implies an integrity of mind, body and action accompanied by some awareness of the nature of these connections in the broader social context." Our bodies and the sensations we feel are with us at all times, yet these sensations are often not part of our consciousness. When we are ill or in pain, our attention is drawn to what our body already knows (Stuckey, 2009). For example, most of the time I don't think about having a nose or the ability to breathe freely. When I have a cold and my nasal passages are blocked, suddenly breathing is all I can think about. According to Ortega y Gasset (1969), there are certain truths that we come to rely on even though we may not have immediate conscious access to them.

> When we discover them for the first time, it seems to us that we have always known them, but had not noticed them; there they were before us, but veiled and covered.... [P]erhaps truth is no more than discovery, the lifting of a veil, or a cover from what was already there and on which we were counting. (p. 50)

Damasio (1999, p. 4) defined *consciousness* as "an organism's awareness of its own self and surroundings." We come into consciousness first through our bodies. "Consciousness emerges when . . . the story of an object can be told using the universal nonverbal vocabulary of body signals . . . from that moment on we begin to know" (pp. 30–31).

Stanage's phenomenological model (1987) includes feeling, experiencing and what he called *consciousing*. Feelings are prereflective. We have feelings and sensations before we are consciously aware of them. Feelings are not yet knowledge, but they are the foundation for knowledge. Experiencing includes both feeling and embodiment. Stanage coined the term *consciousing*, which he used as a verb. Consciousing, or the process of becoming conscious, encompasses both feeling and experiencing and involves reflection and action or praxis. Embodied knowledge can come from conscious engagement with our bodies such as in yoga or dance (see Chapter Six), or it can emerge from our unconscious states, coming into our awareness through intuitive bodily sensations that give us clues to what we know.

Getting in Touch with Embodied Knowledge

Intuition is often expressed as a "gut feeling" or knowledge that is unexplainable. We just know. As there is no rational explanation for how we know, in Western cultures our intuition is often dismissed or not taken seriously. Sometimes this knowledge is just below the surface of our awareness. Getting into our bodies through artistic forms of expression can be a way to get in touch with this hidden knowledge. For example, Stuckey (2009), searching for a way to understand her diabetes, created metaphors to express what her body intuitively knew. "Expression though metaphor is not only a matter of language, but a powerful way to understand the lived experience of the body" (p. 31).

Dance educator Sherry Shapiro wanted her students to understand the concept of women's silent voices, not only from a conceptual perspective but also from their own experience. She asked them to dance their experience and then reflect on what they learned from their bodies. "The power of drawing upon body-knowledge gave the dancers a new understanding of what this might mean. Rather than their bodies being objects for technical proficiency, they became the vehicle for critical understanding of their lifeworld" (Shapiro and Shapiro, 2002, p. 37).

Butterwick and Lawrence (2009) discussed how telling stories through popular theater can be a way to surface strong emotions, providing a way to discuss difficult subject matter and even "creating alternative realities" through dramatization. Similarly Horsfall and Titchen of Australia (2009) used performance ethnography as a way to analyze and present research data in a collaborative inquiry of rural women. The issues that came forward were those that had been formerly "swept under the carpet and included domestic violence; indigenous issues; suicide; and sexism in family farm transfers. The unsay-able became said" (Horsfall and Titchen, 2009, p. 157).

These examples illustrate how embodying an experience can be a way to make knowledge accessible, particularly knowledge that is painful or undiscussable. While these processes can be powerful tools, societal forces mitigate against them.

Feminism and Resistance: Valuing the Body as a Way of Knowing

"Bodies hold knowledge that is not yet present in our conscious mind" (Butterwick and Lawrence, 2009, p. 37), yet our Western educational systems still privilege cognitive rationality. It is as if we are being educated from the neck up. Focusing primarily on cognitive knowledge while ignoring what the body knows deprives us of fully actualizing ourselves as human beings. According to Clark (2001, p. 84): "We're situated in a culture that has a complex and largely troubled relationship with the body. . . . We live much more comfortably in our heads than in our bodies." Talking about our bodies in educational contexts is largely taboo. Freiler (2008) raised the question as to whether modern civilization has turned us off from embodied knowing. According to Damasio (1999, p. 29), "[W]e sometimes use our minds to hide a part of our beings from another part of our beings." We ignore signals from our bodies and our emotions. Perhaps this is a protective mechanism to avoid confronting painful truths. Shapiro and Shapiro (2002) suggested that the body is often associated with the feminine. They saw feminist discourse as a way to reclaim the body. "The body-subject in rational discourse has suffered the effects of alienation in its denial of sensual existence and concrete social experience and it has truncated the knowledge of objective and subjective worlds" (Shapiro and Shapiro, 2002, p. 29).

Feminist scholarship challenges objective rationality that has long been associated with male domination. As Michelson (1998, p. 217) whimsically put it, "Knowledge practices that characterize modernity began on the day that Rene Descartes severed his body from his head." Much of feminist discourse focuses on problematizing and resisting the Cartesian mind/body split, thus reclaiming the body as a source of knowledge. Women, realizing that their association with the body, sexuality, and bodily functions was the source of their oppression, began to speak honestly about their bodies, using this awareness as teaching and learning tools (Clark, 2001). Once women (and probably men as well) begin to be more aware of their body as a teacher, they "cannot return to their former state of unawareness" (Shapiro and Shapiro, 2002, p. 38). This shift in perspective, while still far from universal, holds the potential for an extended epistemology.

Embodied Pedagogy

What would a pedagogy that holds embodied knowledge in equal esteem with cognitive knowledge look like? This section discusses how educators can learn from their students by paying attention to body language and facilitate embodied activities. It then looks at the role of the body in social activism and offers ideas for getting beyond learner resistance.

Paying Attention to Body Language. Embodied pedagogy starts with becoming aware of nonverbal cues that students are communicating. Do they look confused, bored, or engaged? I can often tell by the raised eyebrows, frowns, or puzzled expressions when students are not tracking with me or when something I've said does not make sense to them. If I pay attention to these nonverbal cues, I can use them as an opportunity to pause, check in, and identify the source of the confusion. If no one raises a question and I just continue on as if nothing happened, I could easily miss a "teachable moment." This is one advantage of the face-to-face classroom as opposed to the newer online models where such confusion can easily go undetected.

Facilitating Embodied Activities. Embodied activities such as performance can "tap into visual, emotional and visceral terrain that is often discouraged or silenced in orthodox academic writing" (Horsfall and Titchen, 2009, p. 158). As discussed, embodying stories through movement, dance, or popular theater can be a way to communicate and make connections to others in ways that are less threatening than expressing them verbally or when the knowledge held in the body is not yet conscious. Embodiment is a form of experiential learning as "our experience of life is inevitably mediated through our bodies" (Shilling, 1993, p. 22).

The Body in Social Activism. According to Parviainen (2010), the body plays a major role in social activist work. She observed that words like *movement* and *mobilization* are often used in social change activities in a metaphoric sense, but she also explored a more literal use of the terms. Parviainen (2010) described examples of what she called "choreographing resistances" (p. 316), where people use their bodies as a way to convey a message in social protests. In addition to making a statement to others, the choreography offered the protestors an opportunity to "confront [their] own moral codes and principles behind [their] spontaneous bodily responses" (p. 327), thus providing another avenue for learning.

Learner Resistance. While embodied pedagogy opens many doors for learning, educators need to acknowledge that not all learners may be comfortable with this extrarational approach to learning, and some may actively resist (Freiler, 2008). In my own adult education practice, I have encountered learners who are less than enthusiastic about engaging in body movement and theater activities, deeming them a waste of time away from "real" (book) learning. I recognize that many adults are just not comfortable in their bodies, and the idea that learning can occur in the somatic domain is still a foreign concept. In these situations I try to gently move people just a small step out of their comfort zones by starting with very nonthreatening exercises, such as bringing awareness to where their tension is held in the body, and gradually moving to more challenging activities. Once they get over their initial embarrassment or discomfort, often they are surprised at how much they can learn by actively engaging their bodies.

Sometimes learner resistance to embodiment may be the result of engrained cultural norms and expectations, self-consciousness due to disability or even the result of prior abuse or violation of physical space. Educators need to be sensitive to these experiences and give learners the opportunity to opt out of certain activities.

Conclusion

Human movement is a way of making sense that cannot occur in any other way. People bring their whole selves and the sum of their embodied and affective lived experiences to the learning environment. To not honor all of these experiences is to dishonor the learners themselves. All ways of knowing are valid; however, cultures around the world as well as American indigenous cultures rely on a much broader spectrum of epistemologies than mainstream Western culture. As adult educators, we need to acknowledge and validate knowing from a variety of cultural perspectives and incorporate those perspectives into our practice.

This chapter explored embodied knowing as it comes into our consciousness, how we can access this knowledge, and how we can reclaim the body as a source of knowing. It also began to paint a portrait of an embodied pedagogy. The portrait is not yet finished. We have a long way to go before embodied knowing is taken seriously in our curriculum and in our practice. It is my hope that this chapter and those that follow will inspire adult educators to help complete the portrait and perhaps even paint community murals at educational sites around the globe.

References

Blanchard, M. *The Rest of the Deer: An Intuitive Study of Intuition.* Portland, Maine: Astarte Shell Press, 1993.

Bloom, B. S. *Taxonomy of Educational Objectives.* New York: Longman, 1956. (Original work published in 1984.)

Butterwick, S., and Lawrence, R. L. "Creating Alternative Realities: Arts-Based Approaches to Transformative Learning." In J. Mezirow and E. W. Taylor (eds.), *Transformative Learning in Practice.* San Francisco: Jossey-Bass, 2009.

Clark, M. C. "Off the Beaten Path: Some Creative Approaches to Adult Learning." In S. Merriam (ed.), *The New Update on Adult Learning Theory.* New Directions for Adult and Continuing Education, no. 89. San Francisco: Jossey-Bass, 2001.

Crowdes, M. S. "Embodying Sociological Imagination: Pedagogical Support for Linking Bodies to Minds." *Teaching Sociology,* 2000, 28, 24–40.

Damasio, A. R. *The Feeling of What Happens.* New York: Harcourt Brace, 1999.

Freiler, T. J. "Learning through the Body." In S. Merriam (ed.), *Third Update on Adult Learning Theory.* New Directions for Adult and Continuing Education, no. 119. San Francisco: Jossey-Bass, 2008.

Gardner, H. *Multiple Intelligences: The Theory in Practice.* New York: Basic Books, 1993.
Horsfall, D., and Titchen, A. "Disrupting Edges-Opening Spaces: Pursuing Democracy and Human Flourishing through Creative Methodologies." *International Journal of Social Research Methodology,* 2009, 12(2), 147–160.
Jung, C. G. (ed.). *Man and His Symbols.* New York: Dell, 1964.
Lawrence, R. L. "Powerful Feelings: Exploring the Affective Domain of Informal and Arts-Based Learning." In J. Dirkx (ed.), *Adult Learning and the Emotional Self.* New Directions for Adult and Continuing Education, no. 120. San Francisco: Jossey-Bass, 2008.
Lawrence, R. L. "The Other Side of the Mirror: Intuitive Knowing, Visual Imagery and Transformative Learning." In C. Hoggan, S. Simpson, and H. Stuckey (eds.), *Creative Expression in Transformative Learning.* Malabar, Fla.: Krieger, 2009.
Lawrence R. L., and Dirkx, J. M. "Teaching with Soul: Toward a Spiritually Responsive Transformative Pedagogy." Paper presented at the 29th Annual Midwest Research to Practice Conference, East Lansing, Michigan, 2010.
Mezirow, J. "Learning to Think Like an Adult." In J. Mezirow and Associates (eds.), *Learning as Transformation: Critical Perspectives on a Theory in Progress.* San Francisco: Jossey-Bass, 2000.
Michelson, E. "Re-Membering: The Return of the Body to Experiential Learning." *Studies in Continuing Education,* 1998, 20(3), 217–232.
Ortega y Gasset, J. *Some Lessons in Metaphysics.* New York: Norton, 1969.
Parviainen, J. "Choreographing Resistances: Spatial-Kinesthetic Intelligence and Bodily Knowledge as Political Tools in Activist Work." *Mobilities,* 2010, 5(3), 311–329.
Shapiro, S., and Shapiro, S. "Silent Voices, Bodies of Knowledge: Towards a Critical Pedagogy of the Body." In S. Shapiro and S. Shapiro (eds.), *Body Movements: Pedagogy, Politics and Social Change.* Cresskill, N.J.: Hampton Press, 2002.
Shilling, C. *The Body and Social Theory.* London: Sage, 1993.
Stanage, S. M. *Adult Education and Phenomenological Research.* Malabar, Fla.: Krieger, 1987.
Stuckey, H. "The Body as a Way of Knowing: Meditation, Movement and Image." In C. Hoggan, S. Simpson, and H. Stuckey (eds.), *Creative Expression in Transformative Learning.* Malabar, Fla.: Krieger, 2009.
Vaughan, F. E. *Awakening Intuition.* New York: Doubleday, 1979.
Webster's New World College Dictionary. 4th ed. Edited by Michael E. Agnes. Hoboken, N.J.: John Wiley & Sons, 2004.

RANDEE LIPSON LAWRENCE is an associate professor of adult and continuing education at National Louis University in Chicago.

This article looks to embodied cognition and embodied cognitive science to explore education for self-care.

Embodied Learning and Patient Education: From Nurses' Self-Awareness to Patient Self-Caring

Ann L. Swartz

My memories of educating patients stretch into my distant personal past when my measles experience at five years of age included receipt of a new doll, complete with removable limb casts, crutches, and stick-on red and yellow dots to indicate infectious disease. My embodied experience of illness, of heat, itch, restless sleeplessness, and nightmares, transformed positively as I was able to talk with my new friend about our shared symptoms and how to manage them. I have been a nurse for 35 years and a nursing educator, and this early expression of connected caring grounds my understanding of what it is to be a patient and what it is to care and to teach. Therefore, I eschew the current fashionable term, *client*, with its one-dimensional consumer overtones, and retain the multidimensional *patient*, more resonant with embodied "being in the world."

Embodied learning became interesting as I noticed in clinical settings that many patients are unable to describe symptoms accurately. Sometimes, experiencing disconnection from the body, they don't notice its messages or think to share them. Body sensations can be misinterpreted when they are linked with old memories, especially of trauma or abuse, or with well-meaning old wives' tales. These factors complicate the situation for clinical diagnosticians and patient educators. When the situation is clearer and patients can notice and verbalize body experience, the health-related teaching they receive is usually less nuanced than their own embodied awareness. Again, my own experience can be instructive.

In the final months of undergraduate nursing, I suffered a minor head injury with major sequelae but no follow-up, because I did not require neurosurgery. I accepted that assessment but found myself living in a new "self." Through trial and error, that self learned to read gradations of *fog* states and apply body interventions that brought relief: many hours of sleep; water, protein, and vegetable juice (because I lost track of when I ate and became hypoglycemic); music to move me into action because I had periods of inertia; horseback riding to restore my sense of self moving through space. These interventions didn't come from a book or a professional or even my own conscious reflection on my situation. My body "suggested" things it desired and I acted.

It was 15 years before medicine confirmed that I had sustained a head injury, not just a concussion, and another four years before it figured out how to treat me. Spontaneous visual imagery of what was happening in my brain heralded the onset of new symptoms. Sleep deprivation turned these into depression. My body told me to run, and the neurochemistry generated by running kept my brain functioning for a time. Caring professionals were available to listen, but I could not speak. Pharmaceuticals gave back my brain, but my body instructed me in healing. Tai chi repatterned connections in my body-mind, eye movement desensitization and reprocessing (EMDR) relieved intrusive thoughts, and Reiki brought a felt sense of bodily reintegration. Close attention to body messages helped me create a tapering medication schedule that avoided the withdrawal that keeps many people on antidepressants. Ten years later, when I noticed changes in my breast that radiology denied, I knew to believe my body, and my breast cancer was diagnosed and treated before it metastasized. True, I teach physical examination, but what I saw and felt that led to my self-diagnosis is available to any person who possesses self-knowledge within the body and can therefore notice changes. Now every day of healing begins with a body scan of sensations and ends with a Reiki self-treatment. I am a true believer in embodied knowing. Helping others to embrace this knowledge, for their own inevitable journey as patient, is a passion.

Definition of *Embodied Learning*

This article is intended as a clear and practical introduction to use of a scientific perspective on embodied learning. Freiler (2008), an adult educator, provides a thorough review of intersecting understandings from social science and phenomenology of how learning occurs through the body. She notes that the terms *embodiment, embodied learning*, and *somatic learning* are often used interchangeably. Recent adult education discourse around embodiment (Jordi, 2011; Su, 2011) engages the concept within challenges to our understanding of experiential learning. This work, theoretical and philosophical, brings existential philosophy to the discussion. Both authors critique the biologic conception of humans embedded inseparably within nature as failing to adequately acknowledge human (species) uniqueness. They sometimes conflate the terms *consciousness* and *embodiment*.

Appropriate for my applied science topic in this article, my definition of embodied learning comes from neuroscience via embodied cognition and embodied cognitive science. This definition, because it is empirically derived and not philosophical or theoretical, can avoid Western and Eastern dichotomizing by encompassing both. All living organisms are assumed to be dynamic learning systems embedded in nature. Those with nervous systems are uniquely embodied according to the organization and capabilities of this system. The following definitions refer to the unique human organism, while not privileging it as more unique than other species.

Embodied learning is a heavily brain-influenced process of emergence and stabilization of patterns of connection (of neurons, sensory data, memories, images, ideas, etc.) over time and space (Kelso, 1995) that arise from the embodied mind. *Embodied mind* is a neurobiologic construction of interconnections among body systems, especially nervous and endocrine systems. Embodied mind arises throughout a lifetime of recursive neurobiologic processes that require interpersonal interactions and emotion to proceed. A primary goal of these processes is to integrate the past, present, and future in achieving embodied mind coherence (Kelso, 1995; Siegel, 2001).

These definitions accept the embodiment hypothesis that states: Intelligence is both made in and realized through physical *actions* on the world (Smith, 2006). Here, *intelligence* is the ability to adapt by fitting behavior and cognition (which is embodied) to the changing context, using slight shifts or radical jumps, all being sourced in the embodied mind. *Embodied cognition* is primarily preconscious (therefore, not conscious), unlanguaged embodied knowing for which mindfulness is the natural state of awareness. In this state the embodied mind characteristically knows itself and reflects on its experience, mostly preconsciously and usually without language (Varela, Thompson, and Rosch, 1991).

Patient Education as Context

According to nurse and patient educator Susan Bastable (2008), over the past few decades, the ideal of patient education has evolved from an illness recovery focus to disease prevention and health promotion, moving beyond the traditional imparting of information to an emphasis on empowering patients. Patient education now strives to engage patient and family, taking into account culture, language, learning style, literacy skills, and readiness to learn. Bastable explained that newly purposed patient education aims to increase competence and confidence for self-management. This sounds consistent with the phenomenological "lived body" perspective. However, the new goal is to promote self-care and optimize patient health by getting patients to change risky behaviors and adopt a healthy lifestyle, then manage their own posthospital and chronic illness care with little supervision. Presumably these behavior changes are mutually desired by patient and practitioner. Attitudes and skills are the objective outcomes. Activity emphasizes creation of teachable moments that motivate interest in learning. Outcomes evaluations determine patient education effectiveness according to adherence to prescribed therapeutic regimens and achievement of therapeutic goals as measured by physiologic markers (Bastable, 2008).

The astute adult educator may wonder how a patient educator assumes the implied humanistic stance while the philosophy and goals remain behavioral and driven by measurable outcomes. We should note that despite talk of independence, empowerment, and self-care, the discussion in mainstream health care does not include helping patients know their *lived bodies* as knowledge sources arising from *being in the world*, nor to increasing self-awareness as a substrate for creating health and self-healing.

A Role for Adult Education

Adult education is just beginning to enter the patient education discussion. Certainly it will be beneficial to bring movement, as one of the arts, into patients' healing from disease processes, as discussed by Stuckey and Nobel (2010). This could be construed as tertiary prevention, or prevention of relapse when disease is already present. And secondary prevention, or screening for early signs of disease, is beginning to include a corporeal element. Adult education can contribute its expertise in many forms of learning to this project. But these efforts are still directly tied to specific disease processes and a medical model. What if we radically redirected patient education toward true primary prevention and health promotion, before any disease process exists, even at the unseen tissue level? Then where would embodied learning fit?

Re-Visioning Patient Education as Embodied Learning for Health

Our neurobiologic definition of embodied learning suggests that the purpose of embodied patient education would be to enhance each person's adaptability to changing contexts through physical action. Because each person's embodied mind is a unique product of life experience, individual learning will also be unique and specific outcomes will vary, but the desired general movement would be toward greater integration of past experience and current capability. Emotion and interpersonal relationship would also be essential elements. Methods would include, but certainly not be limited to, those that promote the mind's return to its natural state of mindful reflective awareness (Siegel, 2010). The formation of new patterns of connection would begin with self-awareness and reconnecting self to one's own body through experiential anatomy (Olsen and McHose, 1998). Developed in dance education, experiential anatomy teaches anatomical facts via dance and yoga movements, mindfulness, and imagery. Because health also includes connection to the world around us and disease begins in points of intersection between the person and environment, embodied patient education for health promotion would also seek to build connection between body and earth (Olsen, 2002). These understandings are sourced in my experience of clinical practice, where I assume that health and educating for health are both related to spirituality and culture; that health is wholeness and interconnectedness, and it emerges within families through their rituals and routines (Swartz and Tisdell, 2008).

I have developed what I refer to as *clinical action pedagogy*, based on Miller and Crabtree's (2005) clinical action research paradigm. The purpose is to move practicing registered nurses to enact health for themselves and their patients, particularly within traumatic settings. Application of this pedagogy to patient education enhances enactment of self-care behaviors. When I educate RN-BS nursing students in clinical courses, I view them as a vulnerable group whose health is constantly affected by their work experiences. Therefore, I conduct primary and secondary preventive, clinical intervention with them via pedagogy. Together, these nurses and I successfully bring the same approach to patient education into our health resource center in public housing.

Clinical Action Pedagogy

Miller and Crabtree (2005) reminded readers that clinical worlds are places where "support is sought, and power is invoked" (p. 631), and sought to restore relationship to the clinical world, also a goal of embodied patient education. Rejecting the body-as-machine metaphor, they embrace "body as organism in ecological context" (p. 616), a metaphor drawn from complexity science and ecological science, as are the definitions of embodied learning presented earlier in this chapter. Guided by the premise that the best questions emerge from the "embodied, embedded, and mindfully lived clinical experience" (p. 609), they created a mixed research methodology that makes extensive use of multiple qualitative methods.

By intentionally creating spaces that discover and witness the telling of clinical stories for knowledge sharing, the method emphasizes that participants, who may also be patients, answer their own questions using appropriate research methods. In studying themselves, "they challenge their own situated knowledge and empower their own transformation" (Miller and Crabtree, 2005, p. 612), calling on multiple ways of knowing about the natural world. Individual and collective knowledge intersect with inner and outer reality in their *participatory wheel of inquiry*, derived from the integrative philosophy of Ken Wilber (1996) and similar to Kemmis and McTaggart's (2003) model of participatory action research.

Consistent with critical, feminist, and transformative adult education pedagogies, this clinical action methodology purposely strives to engage metaphors of the body that challenge the limited biomedical view, and it values the slow knowledge focus on nurturing life over outcomes and instrumental rationality. Slow knowledge is "learning at the speed and scale where all life can participate . . . the democratization of knowledge" (Miller and Crabtree, 2005, p. 618). Miller and Crabtree's (2005) simple three-step process begins by identifying alternative healthy relationships and practices that are already occurring in the community, in line with the concept of *positive deviance* (Pascale, Sternin, and Sternin, 2010) associated with complexity science. After joining with these exemplars, the next step is fostering connections among them for mutual support, following something like Freire's (1970) dialogic process of action and reflection to create empowering connections. The final step is creating solidarity, using connected knowing, through these newly emergent, dynamic networks where new embodied and embedded knowledge can grow.

My adaptation of Miller and Crabtree (2005) to design a clinical action pedagogy incorporates a variety of activities that engage multiple ways of knowing, such as self-administered health assessment instruments that engender reflection and self-awareness; written reflections on early body experience memories and memories of connection with places; experiential anatomy; yoga trance dance; mindfulness derived body awareness exercises; reflective journaling; storytelling about body experiencing in complex clinical situations; and drawing of life-size body maps. Clinical courses within the curriculum emphasize different quadrants of the participatory wheel of inquiry but include activities from all quadrants, and students are taught to recognize these differences. For instance, health assessment education aims not only to teach performance of physical exam skills but to increase personal body awareness that will generate more holistic sensitivity to other embodied beings and enhance self-care in students and, by extension, their patients. As with Miller and Crabtree's (2005) clinical process, this patient education process involves cycles of the patient uncovering his or her body story (health and illness), the educator using self-reflection and intuition to understand the person and that person's story within its context, then mutual decisions about further learning needs and possible courses of action.

Translated to our clinic, the wheel provides structure for program planning (see Figure 1). Reflection is oral or through art rather than written, and self-exam screening skills are taught along with bodily self-awareness. Patient education begins in the educators' increased self-awareness. An underlying unifying academic question is, "What are the complex relationships among our bodies, our lives, our ecological context, and power?"

Figure 1. Wheel of Clinical Action Pedagogy: An Embodied Approach to Learning for Health.

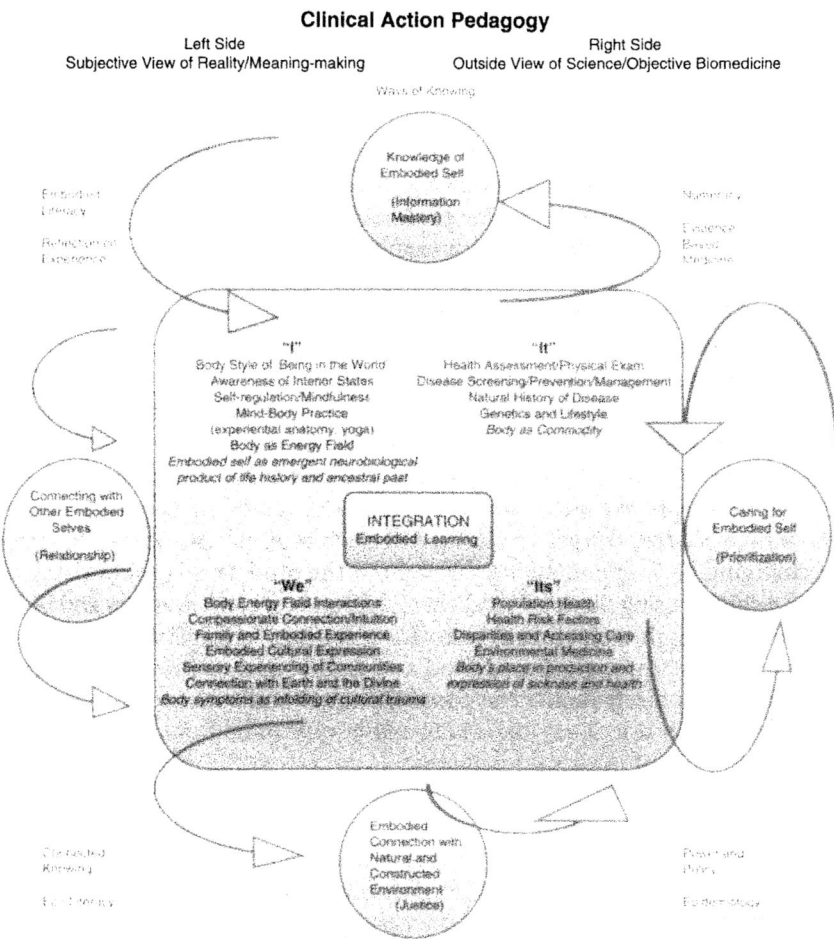

(Miller and Crabtree, 2005, p. 614.) In answering it, patients challenge their own situated knowledge, and transformation becomes possible.

Beginning with yoga dance led by an expert instructor from the community, which is an out-of-the-ordinary experience for most students, assumptions about their body, its experiences, their own performances, and "alternative practitioners" are called into question. Written reflections on the experience build another form of connected knowledge between their own cultural and family knowledge and an external reality of the community. Listening alone to experiential anatomy guided exercises, performing them, and journaling reflectively develops personal knowledge of inner reality and then collective knowledge as insights are shared in class. Completion of quantified self-assessments of factors like sleep deprivation and compassion fatigue generate personal knowledge from the perspective of external reality using quantified data, which when analyzed for the group makes a connection between "I" knowledge and the "we" knowledge of the group. After developing multiple new forms of knowledge through these activities, the experience of telling and listening to three-minute clinical stories in pairs builds interpersonal relationship connections around inner and outer realities. The reflective discussion that follows promotes analysis of issues of justice and disparity within the most external quadrant, where the typical realities of the prevailing health care system are addressed. A final integrative experience is the creation, cooperatively in the group setting, of life-size body maps that are both art and reflection on newly emergent personal and communal knowledge of embodied self.

I am constantly experimenting with new ideas, as are my students. Other activities that have emerged are interactions with music and poetry with attention to body experiencing; mindful eating together in class, followed by reflections on the experience; community walks that engage through photography, conversation with residents, and local eating; experimenting with diet changes, walking and breathing, followed by reflections on changing body experiencing throughout the process; self-monitoring of stress response using Biodots® and changing states of consciousness and body awareness in high-tech clinical simulation settings; engagement with each others' cultures through shared food and games; and learning, practicing, and reflecting on self-Reiki. The possibilities are endless.

Embodied Clinical Action Pedagogy Outcomes

My dissertation research (Swartz, 2010) on the formation of new patterns of connection through learning with this embodied clinical action pedagogy revealed that we all possess unique personal styles of being in the world, through our bodies. These styles show up in body memory stories, as do our histories of trauma, and this body style continues to reappear as we engage in new embodied learning. We will all learn something different, and via a different trajectory, while engaging in the same embodied learning practice. We tend to fear being watched as we "perform" body learning, but practice with group learning moves us beyond this. Personal histories of interpersonal violence call for a greater sense of control in these settings. All persons make sense of new embodied learning as they need to, both in their current context and in relation to their early body memories. Overall, the movement is toward new connections with self experienced as interior awareness, the exercise of new self-care practices, use of movement before turning to medicine for minor pain, and greater comfort in the work setting. In this professional setting, some learners feel more confidence; others less arrogance; others more empathy with patients' embodied experience, more awareness of wholeness and the big picture; and they become more able to act as advocates.

This pedagogy is useful for nurses, but what about patients? Equivalent possibilities for patients include enhanced awareness of embodied knowledge that they could use to promote their own health. Patients would know how a system in balance feels and looks and how health feels and looks, for them, as unique individuals in the world. They would also know how connection and disconnection feel: connection with self, others, the environment, and the divine. Being more connected with their own bodies, they could know through personal experience the meanings of twinges and pain other than as mysterious signs of illness. Patients could also increase their self-confidence in having multiple ways of responding to body messages, beyond ignoring them or passively turning to health care experts. By knowing the value of recognizing emotions and regulating affective responsiveness, their self-regulation ability would increase and relationships could benefit. Remembering and writing one's body memory stories and stories of connectedness to place and drawing body maps contributes to a sense of unique personal identity as a whole person. At the whole-body level, gaining learning confidence in one's ability to read the environment and respond to it effectively supports confidence in one's ability to survive.

Conclusion

This chapter presented a neurobiologic understanding of embodied learning to bridge adult education to the science-driven world of health care. It shared a well-studied pedagogy of embodied education that can be applied to develop embodied patient education. Finally, it suggested a vision of patient education sourced in personal embodied awareness as a most appropriate means of achieving truly empowered patients capable of self-care. Adult education is well positioned to help make this vision a reality. I hope this chapter will inspire a few practitioners to do just that.

References

Bastable, S. B. *Nurse as Educator: Principles of Teaching and Learning for Nursing Practice* (3rd ed.). Sudbury, Mass.: Jones and Bartlett, 2008.
Freiler, T. J. "Learning Through the Body." In S. Merriam (ed.), *Third Update on Adult Learning Theory*. New Directions for Adult and Continuing Education, no. 119. San Francisco: Jossey-Bass, 2008.
Freire, P. *Pedagogy of the Oppressed*. New York: Continuum, 1970.
Jordi, R. "Reframing the Concept of Reflection: Consciousness, Experiential Learning, and Reflective Learning Practices." *Adult Education Quarterly*, 2011, 61(2), 181–197.
Kelso, J.A.S. *Dynamic Patterns: The Self-Organization of Brain and Behavior*. Cambridge, Mass.: MIT Press, 1995.

Kemmis, S., and McTaggart, R. "Participatory Action Research." In J. K. Denzin and Y. S. Lincoln (eds.), *Strategies of Qualitative Inquiry* (2nd ed.). Thousand Oaks, Calif.: Sage, 2003.

Miller, W. L., and Crabtree, B. F. "Clinical Research." In N. K. Denzin and Y. S. Lincoln (eds.), *The Sage Handbook of Qualitative Research* (3rd ed.). Thousand Oaks, Calif.: Sage, 2005.

Olsen, A. *Body and Earth: An Experiential Guide.* Lebanon, N.H.: University Press of New England, 2002.

Olsen, A., and McHose, C. *BodyStories: A Guide to Experiential Anatomy.* Lebanon, N.H.: University Press of New England, 1998.

Pascale, R. T., Sternin, J., and Sternin, M. *The Power of Positive Deviance: How Unlikely Innovators Solve the World's Toughest Problems.* Boston: Harvard Business Press, 2010.

Siegel, D. J. "Toward an Interpersonal Neurobiology of the Developing Mind: Attachment Relationships, 'Mindsight,' and Neural Integration." *Infant Mental Health Journal,* 2001, 22(1–2), 67–94.

Siegel, D. J. *Mindsight: The New Science of Personal Transformation.* New York: Bantam, 2010.

Smith, L. B. "Movement Matters: The Contributions of Esther Thelen." *Biological Theory,* 2006, 1(1), 87–89.

Stuckey, H. L., and Nobel, J. "The Connection Between Art, Healing, and Public Health: A Review of Current Literature." *American Journal of Public Health,* 2010, 100(2), 254–263.

Su, Y. "Lifelong Learning as Being: The Heideggerian Perspective." *Adult Education Quarterly,* 2011, 61(1), 57–72.

Swartz, A. L. "Embodied Learning and Trauma in the Classroom and in Practice." In P. Gandy and others (eds.), *Proceedings of the 51st Adult Education Research Conference.* Sacramento, Calif.: Sacramento State University, 2010.

Swartz, A. L., and Tisdell, E. J. "A Spiritually Grounded and Culturally Responsive Approach to Health Education." In M. A. Perez and R. R. Luquis (eds.), *Cultural Competence in Health Education and Health Promotion.* San Francisco: Jossey-Bass, 2008.

Varela, F. J., Thompson, E., and Rosch, E. *The Embodied Mind: Cognitive Science and Human Experience.* Boston: MIT, 1991.

Wilber, K. *A Brief History of Everything.* Boston: Shambhala Publications, 1996.

ANN L. SWARTZ is an instructor of nursing and affiliate assistant professor of adult education at Penn State University-Harrisburg.

Valuing and validating embodied learning in the workplace makes space for individual learning and transformation and can increase organizational capacity for innovation, learning, and change.

Embodied Learning at Work: Making the Mind-set Shift from Workplace to Playspace

Pamela Meyer

> It is highly possible that what is called "talented behavior" is simply a greater individual capacity for experiencing.
> —Spolin, 1999, p. 1

Umpqua Bank, a rapidly growing community bank in the Northwest, starts each day with a playful "motivational moment" that can include anything from a rousing game of marshmallow dodge ball to a Rolling Stones dance party; an innovative apparel company encourages employees to organize spontaneous events for themselves and their customers like a soap box derby for grown-ups; and a high-end toy company provides improvisation training to everyone in the organization from the chief executive officer to the marketing and warehouse teams (Meyer, 2010). Umpqua Banks's executive vice president of cultural enhancement, Barbara Baker, describes the value of their embodied strategies:

> I can't describe any more than people seem lighter. And it just sets the tone for the rest of the day, and we do it every day. [It's] just seeing people smile or you go to their desk and people say "thank you" more often. They're more conscious of other people around them. I think that is so important . . . . [When] I walk by somebody's desk in career strategies, . . . I say, "Well, we got you [with a flying marshmallow] this morning!" Now, if we didn't have those moments I'd walk by them with my head down and keep going to see Ray

[Umpqua's CEO] or to the ladies' room or the lunchroom. It creates opportunities to create memories, and it creates opportunities to find more ways to communicate with each other. (Meyer, 2010, p. 167)

While these are just a few of many examples of lively, playful, whole-person engagement and embodied learning in the workplace, they are unfortunately the rare exception rather than the rule. One reason for this rarity took root in childhood; most of us were socialized to believe that work and play are incompatible. Another reason is grounded in the largely operational purpose of the workplace. The very word *organization* comes from the Greek *organon*, meaning "tool." The purpose of most organizations is outcomes—the products and services they sell or provide, not the opportunities they create for employee learning and transformation. A singular focus on the functional, operational purpose of the workplace can easily overlook the complexity of the social networks and the relational space in which meaning is made as well as a core site of much significant learning and experience, the body. Another unintended consequence of the emphasis on operational outcomes is that learning and development strategies are often designed solely to enhance productivity and efficiency. Such goal-oriented approaches can limit the human capacity for play and the innovation, learning, and change it fosters.

Making Room for the Play of New Ideas

Organizational learning and transformation and attainment of organizational goals are not at odds. Those who value and consciously integrate whole-person and whole-body strategies in their formal and informal learning practices encourage people to bring their whole selves, including their emotional, physical, and spiritual life, to work (Barry and Hazen, 1996).

As organizations embrace and understand the value of whole-person engagement, they begin to make a mind-set shift from one of workplace, which emphasizes outcomes and routines, to one of playspace, which reclaims play as essential to organizational success (Meyer, 2010). *Playspace* means the space quite literally for the play of new ideas, for people to play new roles, for more play in the system, and for improvised play.

This shift in mind-set is tied to another key organizational benefit. Without the intrinsic motivation to do so, people do not expend discretionary effort, challenge cherished assumptions, innovate, or persevere through challenging obstacles, let alone take the initiative to respond creatively to unexpected and unplanned events or co-create novel solutions (Amabile, 1996). Intrinsic motivation is sparked by the lived experience of meaning and embodied awareness. This experience along with expanded self-concepts and capacities becomes possible when all organizational members, including leaders, facilitators, and participants, share responsibility for creating the space for it (Meyer, 2009).

Perhaps in part because of the outcomes to which they are held accountable, learning and development practitioners are just beginning to imagine what is possible if embodied learning, and practices that facilitate it, are validated and valued in the workplace. What if the body was valued as a site of learning in organizations? What knowledge would become valid? What capacities and talents might emerge? What learning and transformation becomes possible?

Embodied Learning in Action

Mightybytes, a small digital media firm in Chicago, is discovering some important answers to these questions by embracing informal, embodied learning at work. Its learning strategies do not come from corporate executives, human resource professionals, or learning and development practitioners; they emerge intrinsically from the values, commitments, and passions of the participants themselves.

In conducting research at Mightybytes, I learned that at the core of the organization is a commitment to the local community and to sustainable business practices, sometimes called the triple bottom line: people, planet, and profits (Elkington, 1997). Three regular activities exemplify this commitment:

1. Weekly "Lunch and Learn" sessions. One person shops the neighborhood farmers' market, then creates and prepares a lunch from the ingredients in collaboration with the team while a second person prepares a lunchtime presentation on an emerging digital media trend or technology.
2. Friday afternoon "Mightybrew" sessions. Every few weeks, the crew members, as they call themselves, work together in the company kitchen brewing beer for their own and clients' enjoyment.
3. Biking. Mightybites' crew members also regularly bike to work. They recently organized a ride in which they rode throughout the city, picking up the entire team for a group ride to the office. Several Mightybytes members also participate in the Climate Ride, which raises money to support a sustainable future.

Each of these practices contributes to the overall health and well-being of the organization and generates important new knowledge and possibilities. For many participants, the embodied learning and engagement each strategy fosters stand out. The web developer at Mightybytes, Bryan Zera, reflected in a personal interview:

> At the moment when you're participating in brewing beer or riding bikes with your coworkers or doing a Lunch and Learn, anything collaborative [the idea] is that "this is not just a job." This is a place that's dedicated to doing things

that help keep you interested in wanting to be in this physical space.... So those extra things just serve to really keep you invested in what's going, in the work that's going on here by giving you an opportunity to play here as well.

Organizations that value and make space for embodied learning enjoy a number of benefits. Participants develop individual and group capacities that enhance their enjoyment and effectiveness at work. They also generate important relational knowledge (Park, 1999), renew their energy and engagement, and improve collaboration.

Relational Knowledge. Zera described his experience as feeling "like I know my coworkers better when we do stuff like this together." Others commented that they feel more comfortable asking for help because of the bonds they build through these embodied and whole-person experiences. Designer Joy Burke shared that "a common theme for all of us is that we don't want to let each other down." Unlike representational or instrumental knowledge, relational knowledge is embedded in the relationships themselves and is gained through shared experience.

Energy and Engagement. Zera also reflected on the power of activities like the group ride to ignite the team. "I remember the energy being really high that day." He also shared how on brewing days, there is a heightened sense of engagement:

> ... because it further forces you to get up and do other things and take a mental break from the task at hand. And it is really nice, too, because the brewing process like the boil [a stage in brewing] has sort of predefined chunks of time. So you have to let it boil for an hour total. So it is broken up by the addition of ingredients that lend itself to natural breaks in your work where you would accomplish a chunk and then have to get up and attend to something else.

For Zera, the playful diversion of biking and brewing has a direct effect on the attitude of play he brings to his work.

Improved Collaboration. Whether biking, brewing, or cooking together, the embodied learning extends into the rest of the workday. Burke finds power in the metaphor of their embodied learning practices "that's kind of symbolic for the way that we try to work in our day-to-day job too. And then the same goes with brewing. No one drops the ball, we all try to make sure that everything's covered, someone knows what's going on and what's next; we work the same way too."

Bill Dagiantis, the business development specialist, described in an interview how Mightybytes' embodied strategies improved everyone's ability to think on his or her feet: "You've got someone cooking and you have someone either standing at the white board, because it's in the same room, or grabbing something out of the fridge or pouring a drink and they're still kind of chatting business while trying to cook the meal. It helps us improve our ability to . . . think on the fly."

Embodied Transformative Learning. As a facilitator, when using embodied strategies such as improvisational games, I have witnessed and documented many examples of what I now believe to be "embodied transformative learning," in which the transformation came not in the form of a perspective shift (Mezirow & Associates, 1990) but through a shift in the embodied experience as adults co-create the space in which it is safe to participate with their whole selves and become aware of and engage their whole bodies as well as their emotions, intuition, humor, environment, and each other (Meyer, 2009). As participants learning improvisation begin experiencing themselves differently, their former self-beliefs can be challenged and eventually begin to shift as they embrace and lived into their expanded capacities.

It's Not Like Work. Additionally, as I studied adults' descriptions of their experiences learning improvisation (Meyer, 2006a, 2006b), I noticed a recurring theme: "It's not like work." For many, their day-to-day lived experience at work contrasted greatly with their experience learning improvisation. Lisa's experience participating in improvisation games exemplifies an important way that embodied learning can reenergize participants before, after, and during the workday. Mainemelis and Ronson (2006) make the distinction between play as diversion and play as engagement. In Lisa's case, her energizing experience of play as diversion restored her so that she could engage in her work more playfully. She told me:

> I was surprised at how energized I became during the exercise. . . . Stimulating the imagination is a transforming experience for me. Because all the garbage from the day is dissipating. Walking at the different paces and imagining various scenarios left me feeling aware and refreshed, as when I replenish my body with food or wake up and have a steaming cup of coffee and awaken to the day. It really did not take much time for me to feel the effect either . . . . I came in tired and worn out from work and started to come back to life and feeling renewed. Better than coffee and certainly more fun! (Meyer, 2006a, p. 2)

Christina described a similar experience of the workday "slowly evaporating" during a relaxation exercise: "I kept telling myself, okay, soon this feeling will pass and I will feel the energy that we create in this classroom. I was not disappointed. As soon as we did the 'here and now time' I feel like all the anxiety just slowly evaporates out of my body little by little" (Meyer, 2006b, p. 138).

Embodied learning strategies, whether they occur in the classroom or the kitchen, generate significant value for individual participants and the organization as a whole. Workplaces that afford people the opportunity to be authentic and invite whole-person, whole-body engagement are likely to be places where workers expend discretionary, creative energy for the good of the organization.

Implications for Practitioners

How can we who practice and participate in organizational systems share responsibility for creating the space for embodied learning at work? The first step is to ensure that embodied learning and the knowledge it generates are valued at all levels of the organization. For many, validating embodied learning requires a mind-set shift from workplace to playspace (Meyer, 2010). Rather than approaching this as a cognitive shift, practitioners can take a whole-person approach and begin experimenting with the use of several embodied practices to discover what emerges that could be considered organizationally "valid." What do you observe happening during the experiences? What, if anything, is shifting in the group dynamic? What do participants describe, and what benefits do they report? The answers to these questions may very likely include valuable benefits for the organization and for the participants. In this section I suggest some ways that leaders, facilitators, and participants can share responsibility for creating the playspace in which embodied learning can occur.

Leaders. People who, by formal or informal role, take responsibility for influencing change have some of the most significant influence as they model and reinforce organizational values and behaviors.

Give Permission. The role of giving permission is most impactful when played by organizational leaders. It can often spread to other participants who model and reinforce the behaviors and attitudes most conducive to innovation, learning, and change. Permission givers are often the first to risk sharing a wild idea or personal experience, to ask a provocative question, or otherwise to push beyond the edges of the prevailing norms.

The role of the permission giver is particularly important in organizational settings because individuals are more likely to adjust their behavior to what is considered acceptable behavior than to test cultural norms. I witnessed just such an example of permission giving by leadership when, after a morning of idea generation and collaboration exercises, the sales director of a major manufacturing organization got up to begin her presentation. She began bouncing and giggling as she set up her first slide, which elicited generous laughter and applause from the group. Her playful, embodied spirit invited everyone else to act playfully; it also kept the lively creative collaboration and inquiry in motion during an afternoon of traditionally dry material.

Facilitators. Those who take on the role of formally or informally designing and guiding group and individual learning, inquiry, and collaboration can strongly influence organizational practices and routines and be custodians of the playspace that enables embodied learning.

Invite Embodied Awareness. It is often easiest to facilitate embodied learning when playing the role of the facilitator. Simple practices such as inviting participants to "get back in their bodies" by standing up and taking a few deep relaxation breaths and drawing their awareness to their physical, mental, and emotional states can open the door to embodied learning. Repeating this invitation, along with a range of opportunities for people to get up and move, change their point of view, and disrupt their habituated experience of the body, often brings with it new awareness of and appreciation for embodied learning. Improvisation games are particularly effective in engaging embodied learning and freeing people from self-consciousness. Participants can also be invited to express this awareness through nontraditional means. For example, rather than asking participants to share their insights through written or spoken reflection, facilitators can invite them to draw an image or compose and perform a short movement phrase expressing their current embodied state. These practices may seem outside of the comfort zone (and culture) for many organizational participants; often, however, a confident facilitator can co-create a safe and playful space for people to explore beyond the familiar.

Disrupt the Routine. Similar disruptions and renewed awareness can come from providing informal and situated learning experiences and stretch assignments that pull people out of their comfort zone. Facilitators, coaches, and managers who regularly inquire about what people are aware of thinking, feeling, and doing during these experiences can help attune workers to the learning that is available at the site of the body. For example, awareness of increasing energy when solving a complex customer problem can be a sign of engagement and, with further reflection, can lead to the appreciation and development of a previously untapped talent.

Participants. Anyone who, while not in a formal role of authority, is responsible for engaging in and co-creating the success of the shared learning or collaboration experience determines the ultimate possibilities that emerge from embodied learning. Everyone in the workplace, regardless of his or her formally assigned role, is a participant. Especially when not charged with leading or facilitating organizational processes, participants have the biggest impact on the day-to-day opportunities for embodied learning. Here are two simple participant practices that can enhance embodied learning.

Breathe. Taking two or three deep breaths throughout the day to notice your current embodied state is a wonderful way not only to relax and return to the present moment but to pay attention to *all* of the information, learning, and insight available to you.

Inquire. Inquiring about colleagues' embodied states may seem awkward at first, but asking "What are you feeling in response to this?" and even the more risky "Is your body giving you any information?" can serve as an invitation to attune to the body as a site of learning in a way that simply asking "What do you think?" will not.

Conclusion

Creating playspace for and fostering practices that allow people at all levels of the organization to engage their whole selves and their whole bodies can set the stage for people to play new roles and discover new capacities. When learning and development strategies are too tightly linked to organizational operations and outcomes, the most powerful possibilities for engagement, innovation, and the play of new possibilities can be constrained or missed altogether. Those who risk stepping out of their comfort zone and into their bodies not only enjoy their own personal rewards; they might also give permission to others to explore new frontiers in their own learning and development with previously unimagined organizational value.

References

Amabile, T. M. *Creativity in Context*. Boulder, Colo.: Westview Press, 1996.

Barry, D., and Hazen, M. A. "Do You Take Your Body to Work?" In D. M. Boje, R. P. Gephart, Jr., and T. J. Thatchenkery (eds.), *Postmodern Management and Organization Theory*. Thousand Oaks, Calif.: Sage, 1996.

Elkington, J. *Cannibals with Forks: The Triple Bottom Line of 21st Century Business*. San Francisco: Wiley, 1997.

Mainemelis, C., and Ronson, S. "Ideas Are Born in Fields of Play: Towards a Theory of Play and Creativity in Organizational Settings." *Research in Organizational Behavior: An Annual Series of Analytical Essays and Critical Reviews*, 2006, 27, 81–131.

Meyer, P. "Learning Space and Space for Learning: Adults' Intersubjective Experiences of Improvisation." Paper presented at the Adult Education Research Conference, University of Minnesota, May 20, 2006a.

Meyer, P. "Learning Space and Space for Learning: Adults' Intersubjective Experiences of Improvisation." Unpublished doctoral dissertation, Fielding Graduate University, 2006b.

Meyer, P. "Learning Space/Work Space: Can We Make Room for Transformative Learning at Work?" In B. Fisher-Yoshida, K. D. Geller, and S. A. Schapiro (eds.), *Innovations In Transformative Learning: Space, Culture, and the Arts*. New York: Peter Lang, 2009.

Meyer, P. *From Workplace to Playspace: Innovating, Learning and Changing Through Dynamic Engagement*. San Francisco: Jossey-Bass, 2010.

Mezirow, J., and Associates (eds.). *Fostering Critical Reflection in Adulthood: A Guide to Transformative and Emanicpatory Learning*. San Francisco: Jossey-Bass, 1990.

Park, P. "People, Knowledge and Change in Participatory Research." *Management Learning*, 1999, 30(2), 141–157.

Spolin, V. *Improvisation for the Theater*. Evanston, Ill.: Northwestern University Press, 1999.

PAMELA MEYER *teaches at DePaul University's School for New Learning and is president of Meyer Creativity Associates.*

This article highlights four concepts related to embodied knowledge for community awareness: possibilities, risk, collective engagement, and performance.

Embodying Women's Stories for Community Awareness and Social Action

Yolanda Nieves

> You must give birth to your images. They are the future waiting to be born. Fear not the strangeness you feel. The future must enter you long before it happens.
>
> —Rainer Maria Rilke

> Inherent in the creative act is a spiritual, psychic component—one of spiritual excavation, of (ad)venturing into the inner void, extrapolating meaning from it and sending it out into the world. To do this kind of work requires the total person-body, soul, mind, and spirit.
>
> —Gloria Anzaldua

What if knowledge is an energy force? Imagine that this force can live and manifest itself in the cells of our bodies. Imagine that our thoughts and what we learn inhabit the entrails of our being. For months I have struggled to put into words my experience in researching and developing a community education project that has grown to embody a life of its own. This article examines my narrative study investigation manifested in a performance text as a case study on how women embodied repressed knowledge and released it through performance. Selby (2002) wrote: "In a world in which, at one level of presence, everything relates to everything else and, at a deeper level, everything is embedded in everything else, we have to acknowledge that flow, movement and complexity, allied to our limited vision and inability to comprehend and entertain all the questions to ask, make for, at best, provisional knowing" (p. 84). I offer my perspective that provisional or rational knowing that is stored in the intellect is complemented by the knowledge that is permanently stored in the body—if we allow ourselves to be attuned to it.

The process of sharing embodied knowledge can be described in these ways, among others: the flesh acts as incubator, memory floats in us as an embryo, voice becomes the midwife to knowledge, and praxis, the life force that distributes knowledge. The idea that knowledge is stored in the body and can be transferred to others via performance is being birthed, in academia, as a legitimate ideology. I believe that acknowledging embodied knowledge as a vehicle for adult education can also act as a healing force for the academy.

What we call "gut feelings"—the intuitive or sixth sense—is a type of energy that shifts and grows like the fluidity of an embryonic membrane. Acknowledging this energy can be the force that drives social action. Following the fluidity of the intuitive helped me immerse myself in a community action project that became (and still is) a life-altering experience for me. A narrative inquiry study on the identity construct of second-generation Puerto Rican women was conceived in my small kitchen in an animated discourse with an inner circle of sister-daughters. That was the beginning of a profound understanding of how our bodies do not just house our intellect but can be the axis where past, present, memory, and (r)evolution intersect. Through my study I became a witness to the tension embodied in voice, narrative, text, and performance. This tension seeks to be released.

Embodying the Possibilities

It is my position that the body, like a container, holds historical, cultural, and political memory in organic ways we strain to explain. It is difficult to pinpoint how the body chooses to perform stories. Some people call it intuition; others may attribute it to an organic process that happens spontaneously at a specific moment in time. When I embarked on my study to investigate the lived experiences of second-generation Puerto Rican women, the idea of a performance came from my love of poetry, theater, and community. Even before my investigation had taken on its framework, I had engaged in an initial collaboration with my sister, who is also a poet and actress. A script that we had cowritten was accepted by a prominent theatrical contest. Surprised by its acceptance, my two daughters, my sister, and I began to rehearse the script. I invited my dissertation adviser to join us for the event.

After the performance, I was astonished by the positive feedback from the audience. I agreed, after some coaxing by my dissertation adviser, to consider embodying the data I would collect for my investigation. In that way, it would become a community education project espousing social action. On a frigid afternoon in January, I again gathered my daughters and sister in what was now my sacred circle of women and my first set of collaborators, in an attempt to critically examine issues related to identity and marginalization that second-generation Puerto Rican women have experienced but felt compelled to silence due to colonialist, racist, sexist, and patriarchal structures. As the afternoon turned into evening, our bodies maneuvered through physical and vocal reactions that indicated the beginning of a collective liberatory educational project. That day I physically experienced how the body is indeed a terrain of struggle. My lips trembled as began to share the truth of my experiences with marginalization. My facial muscles twitched, while the palpitation of my heartbeat drummed in my ears. Short, spiked breaths leading into deep breaths intertwined my testimony. We physically interrupted each other with simultaneous conversations arising all at one time, standing, pacing, eyes opening wide as we shared our ideas, at times finishing each other's sentences and at other times enmeshing our grief within each other's arms. Our flesh gave way to voice. Voice led us to the intersection of collective strength and painful truth telling, the breaking through the wall of "Other," and migrating into the land called *Subject*.

Embodying the Risk

The five women I interviewed for my study provided me with stories that they had carried in their bodies for decades. The interviewees gave me their stories based on the fact that they "knew" me. In this particular cultural context, to "know" me meant that they saw me as a member of their community through my locality—I had lived in the neighborhood all of my life. It also meant that they "knew" me through my family's decades-old connection to the neighborhood's religious, cultural, and political history. I was one of them—I had insider status—and they trusted me.

I used critical race theory (CRT), Latino critical race theory (LatCrit), and critical race feminism (CRF) to guide my analysis of the women's narratives. CRT (Bell, 1992) examines how race is socially constructed and how racism is systematically and normally incorporated into our systems, particularly in the U.S. legal system. LatCrit and CRF emerged from CRT. LatCrit scholars such Delgado and Stefancic (2000) contributed to the concerted movement by a group of Latino legal scholars who sought to address the racial, ethnic, and language discrimination Latinos encountered in the United States, challenging the notion that Latinos/as experience racism the same way African Americans do. LatCrit seeks to move beyond the black-white binary. CRF scholars, such Anzaldua (1999) and Wing (2003), focus on the multilayered, gendered marginalization of women. CRF brings to the forefront the agency of gender and anti-essentialism of women. All of these frameworks use the idea of counterstorytelling—stories that diverge from the grand narratives and the normed historical truths purported by the dominant culture. Counterstorytelling seeks to intervene by centering the lived experiences of people who have had little or no voice. Therein lies the power of these frameworks.

The concept of counterstorytelling, framed by CRT and CRF, symbiotically fell into place with the project. Storytelling is a communal act. Text needs voices, bodies, and gestures to give birth to stories. Thus, a broader understanding of the unwritten and undocumented events that occur but hold no importance to dominant society can occur through remembering and sharing stories. For marginalized people—in my case, second-generation Puerto Rican women—to tell stories is to embody and share specific undocumented truths. Counterstories also implicate the political structures that oppress individuals. They have an ability to expose all of us to alternative ways of thinking; shared knowledge, embodied in those who seem "invisible" in our society, can transform us. For my purposes, the counterstory shone a light on history and on people who would otherwise have been forgotten or erased.

The summer that I began to read and reread the interview transcripts, the stories took on a life of their own inside my own body. I became every woman I interviewed as I drank their lived experiences. Every time I reviewed the transcripts, I lived every moment of oppression, marginalization, alienation, and "othering." I felt my body revel in small triumphs of subversive and trangressive acts each woman performed to maintain her dignity. My entire body engaged in a physical and spiritual shape-shifting. I traveled back and forth through "narrative" time. During countless instances, my body could hold no more. I would drag myself to bed long before the sun went down, exhaustion overtaking me.

Throughout that time the stories and I became a living co-performance; as I read and internalized the stories, the data became a living form inside of me. I liken the stories to an embryo; the narratives, like a living cell, joined other cells, then dividing, forming one larger body that would become the performance text.

Most challenging were the decisions that had to be made on what parts of the stories were to be included and excluded. How would the women's words and their intentions come to life through the text? The text, out of context, could be a weapon against the integrity of the women and of the research. I decided to exclude parts of the narratives that would exploit or further marginalize the women or were not related to my research questions. My embodiment of the women's narratives and the writing of the text became an act of thinking with the heart. And my heart, joined with the interviews, demanded poetry, song, and body movement—all ways that a body can re-present knowledge.

As scholars struggle to understand how the body knows and learns, I am heartened by the academy awakening to feminist research. Denzin

(2005) stated, "Scholars must develop culturally responsive research practices that locate power within indigenous communities" (p. 936). I would like to add that culturally responsive researchers need to trust the location of knowledge in their bodies.

Embodying Collective Engagement

The embodiment of knowledge can also be found in collective engagement. Collective engagement is a pedagogy of necessity for adult education projects. As soon as I had made the decision to perform the text, many preliminary preparations had to be made, much as a mother prepares for the birth of her child. First, for the text to be a living document, it must be performed. For months I had attended conferences, and gone to public readings where "open mike" opportunities allowed me to test run the script and probe the audience for reactions to the performance text. I wanted to gauge audience reactions and responses.

Some of these questions guided my writing: Did the audience grasp the story? Were they able to absorb the profoundness of a racial incident in the text? Was my interpretation of the stories strong enough to incite a consciousness raising experience? Had I done justice to the intimacy that had been shared with me by my interviewees? Would I have to perform the text alone?

In addition to my doctoral courses, I had also completed a three-week workshop on how to perform a one-woman show—just to ensure that I had some kind of framework and method for the presentation of the text. My original intent was to perform it alone.

However, word had gotten around in the Humboldt Park community (a largely Puerto Rican neighborhood in Chicago) through a neighborhood writing group that I had written some sort of script. A young single mother, also a poet, had been in attendance at several of the probes I had conducted around Chicago's poetry venues. We began a friendship due to her immediate connection with the stories. I shared the story of my investigation and challenges with her. Finding a space for the performance of the text was difficult. Where could this performance take place? I had written the text to be a community education project, so a university setting would not do. I joked that I might have to perform it in a rented storehouse or garage due to the lack of performance spaces in Humboldt Park. Another concern was that the text was rather long, about 90 pages. Could I memorize the entire script? These issues would be just the first hurdles I would have to jump.

The young single mother and I had acquaintances in a writing group, and she shared her enthusiasm with some of the women there. Enter my second set of collaborators—five women, all volunteers who loved the arts—who stepped forward to participate in the project. Once again, my kitchen became the space where my new collaborators came together with my sister and daughters to help birth the voices in the script. In that intimate space, the women, whom I will call co-performers, embraced the stories as their own. As they read the script, they began to raise their hands to ask questions or shouted out their desire to represent the voices in various scenes. They were becoming translators of embodied knowledge, using their own repressed voices as vehicles to give life to the narratives. The co-performers became a fluid membrane that used their own re-membering and bodies to share collective history.

At the same time, I was introduced to a young producer who was looking to feature Latino/a artists in a new venue. In a five-minute meeting, he gauged my enthusiasm and booked us for a four-day run at the Chicago Center for the Performing Arts, a 140-seat theater complete with a tech booth, lights, sound, a public relations manager, and a stage. Goodman (2002) described circumstances that come together as being "an age where there is new intimacy between all living beings and the cosmos and a far more profound understanding of our responsibilities and mutuality" (p. 196). I'm not sure what triggered such positive outcomes for this adult education project except to say that there was synergy.

The co-performers and I decided on a name for the group: the Vida Bella Ensemble, which means beautiful life. Also, I had finally settled on a name for the performance text: *The Brown Girls' Chronicles: Puerto Rican Women and Resilience*. In this way, the space of our bodies had found a place to perform the narratives. Before long, the idea of a larger production was blossoming in the metaphorical wombs of the co-performers. My own resilience was growing too. It was exciting to know that the narratives that were bequeathed to me, which in turn were nurtured by the co-performers, were now going to belong to the community.

Embodying the Performance

My consistency in keeping a journal as field notes helped me cope with the mounting pressures of the group dynamics, the rehearsals, and other technical issues. There was also a stirring in the community. No one but the women had read the script, but there was consternation on various community fronts. Two weeks before the performance, I wrote the following in my journal:

February 27, 2009

...every single detail of this performance has been questioned by someone—but because I have my theoretical framework I have a clear direction of where I am going. The music, the playbill . . . the issue of money and tickets (the ticket price is only $5.00 and the producer cannot understand why we do not charge more), and some community leaders think that the women do not have enough talent to perform. Our integrity was questioned by some churches. What do I want to say about this? I want to say I'm ecstatic—happy beyond my wildest dreams! If even for a little while, this project has interrupted history.

Even as I reread my field notes, I am astounded by my bravado and naiveté. Nevertheless, there were some casualties along the way. One of the co-performers dropped out, disturbed by the narratives related to sexual identity issues. I had to let another ensemble member go when her inability to concentrate, remember her lines, and arrive on time began to hinder the performance. A week before the show, we were down to seven women. The stress was mounting.

Several of the co-performers in the ensemble began to outwardly struggle with their bodies and body images. One ensemble member couldn't come in on time in a duet. Another constantly froze in the middle of her lines, and yet another struggled with the idea that her husband and coworkers were not "taking her seriously." The women experienced body aches, weight gain, weight loss, and timing issues in the group choreo-poems. One co-performer who had exceptional physical beauty struggled to break out of her "Marilyn Monroe" persona to embody the experience of an incarcerated woman. I believed that these were all metaphorical incantations of the co-performers' own struggle with identity issues and the marginalization they themselves had experienced. As well as performing and directing the text, I had to coach, coax, and even scold the women at times to get them ready for the performance. Yet as we embodied the stories, the co-performers began to tutor each other, recounting their own resurfaced memories, exchanging books and articles, and sharing techniques on how to move on stage. The Vida Bella Ensemble became our education project within a larger education project. Meanwhile, during rehearsals, as the pain and triumph of the narratives entered our bodies, we would stop to cry and console each other. Our bodies and minds were re-forming themselves to present the text to an excited but questioning community.

I struggled with my own thoughts and fears too. For a month before the performance, I was unable to get a full night's rest. I would get up before dawn, pace, review my lines, meditate, and practice my body movements. Yet on March 5, 2009, the morning of the performance, I wrote:

The stories that have come to life are more real than life itself!

A unique adult educational project was going to be born that night. Everyone would know if I was a "fake" or if my intent had been true. My mind, my body, and my own history with the community would be on stage. Wilcox (2009) stated: "Lived experiences, performance, and bodily intelligence are three interconnected concepts that help us consider and practice embodied ways of knowing in education" (p. 105). I would add that a unifying factor among those three concepts is the collective agency of people coming together to excavate new ways of learning. The audiences would give the performance its final interpretation as they bore witness to the stories and embodied the knowledge we would share with them.

Embodied Ways of Knowing

The four days of performing were incredibly stressful and exhilarating. The question-and-answer period after each performance was what gave me the deepest insight into what the audience had embodied. After the second night of the performance, I wrote:

> This play is stirring up deep emotions in many people, in some great anger. One woman stood up to defend the text while another wanted a history workshop, right then and there.

The most important part of sharing our embodied knowledge was to extend it to the audience. In receiving the performed narratives, the audience absorbed the knowledge embedded in the text given to them by the co-performers. In this way the audience holds the final interpretation of the text. What knowledge and life experiences they know to be true in their lives is cojoined with the stories the actors have interpreted on stage. The audience, by the mere fact of sitting in a particular place, space, and time, takes on the responsibility of interpretation. Each audience member will hear, see, and come away with a different experience. As witnesses to the stories, they all are participants in an embodied experience. The learning, deconstruction, and reconstruction knowledge will happen at various levels. These may be unknown to the co-performers and the writer. Even so, the audience becomes an integral "co-character" of the text.

When the audiences become co-characters of the text, it can cause distress among all the participants. The participation by the audiences led me to deeply ponder what I thought I knew about the script I wrote. In embodying and sharing knowledge, we can unwittingly create new knowledge. My field notes reflect this. In March 2009 I wrote:

> Every evening I went out there [on stage] with the understanding that the audience was a classroom. I knew people would have strong feelings about the text, but never did I imagine that it would stir and invoke such profound responses . . . anger, pride, shame, denial, connections, disconnections, wonder, disbelief . . . I think there was also a sense of hope. At least, I'd like to think so. After doing this, I question everything I perceive. . . . we all do such a great job of creating our own realities that we see right through the very thing that stands before us . . . the undeniable experience of being.

Two years after the debut of *The Brown Girls' Chronicles*, I can say that over five thousand people have seen the performance, coast to coast. Over and over again the questions this case study brought to the forefront for me as an adult educator were: Can the body be a source of learning and a be a source for teaching and healing? Can the sharing of embodied knowledge create community awareness and social action? My answer is an emphatic yes!

Implications for Adult Educators

What I understood through *The Brown Girls' Chronicles* was that embodied knowledge can be a collective social performance where repressed and subjugated truths are transferred from people to people. The co-performers and I were able to reclaim not only our voices through women's stories; we were able to free repressed social, cultural, and political history through our bodies and help the audience to reclaim it too. Our bodies, through performance, rescued subjugated truths and redefined our reality—if only for the time we were on stage. Our bodies acted as tools to interrupt time and became the terrain where a subversive community education project flourished. The narratives we all absorbed intervened on our behalf and contributed to an adult education liberatory project.

I propose that embodying knowledge can also be visualized as a spiral, circular process, situated in the space, place, and time of our bodies. Our bodies—a fluid architectural form—"know" and flow in and out of memory, voice, and praxis if we dare to perform what we know and what we learn. Perhaps, if adult educators continue to stretch the traditional educational processes we employ, then the spirit of knowledge—embodied, contextualized, and performed as an enactment of consciousness—will enhance our practice. To do so, however, our minds and bodies must align ourselves to a commitment of discomfort and respect for what is embedded in us.

To expand our academic rituals and traditions, educators might want to consider talking to each other to find alternative ways to share their research, resources, and knowledge. Involving nonacademic but viably vested community organizations to join educational efforts is a powerful way of opening avenues for research, teaching, and learning. Finding opportunities to share space and time, in and out of academia's regulated time frames, can help to build communities. Last, I pose a question, and perhaps there is no one right answer for it: How can we, as educators, take the existing power structures and reframe inequalities to create a more humane and liberatory way of teaching and learning? Certainly, doing so would embody a lifetime of challenging performances on our parts.

References

Anzaldua, G. A. *Borderlands/La Frontera: The New Mestiza* (2nd ed.). San Francisco: An Aunt Lute Foundation Book, 1999.

Bell, D. *Faces at the Bottom of the Well.* New York: Basic Books, 1992.
Delgado, R., and Stefancic, J. (eds.). *Critical Race Theory: The Cutting Edge* (2nd ed.). Philadelphia: Temple University Press, 2002.
Denzin, N. K. "The Discipline and Practice of Qualitative Research." In N. K. Denzin and Y. S. Lincoln (eds.), *The Sage Handbook of Qualitative Research.* Thousand Oaks, Calif.: Sage, 2005.
Goodman, A. "Transformative Learning and Cultures of Peace." In E. V. O'Sullivan, A. Morrell, and M. A. O'Conner (eds.), *Expanding the Boundaries of Transformative Learning.* New York: Palgrave Macmillan, 2002.
Selby, D. "Expanding the Boundaries of Transformative Learning." In E. V. O'Sullivan, A. Morrell, and M. A. O'Conner (eds.), *Expanding the Boundaries of Transformative Learning.* New York: Palgrave Macmillan, 2002.
Wing, A. K. (ed.). *Critical Race Feminism: A Reader* (2nd ed.). New York: New York University Press, 2003.
Wilcox, H. N. "Embodied Ways of Knowing, Pedagogies, and Social Justice: Inclusive Science and Beyond." *NWSA Journal,* 2009, *21*(2), 104–120.

YOLANDA NIEVES, Ed.D., is an assistant professor at Wilbur Wright College in Chicago. She is also a poet, playwright, and the artistic director of the Vida Bella Ensemble.

This article explores experiential education as the use of direct experience for enhancing social, emotional, and intellectual growth.

Outdoor Experiential Education: Learning Through the Body

Eric Howden

Most people can recall a time when they learned a skill or came to understand an idea while participating in an experience: learning in such a way that the action being taken and the resulting learning outcomes were synonymous. Time spent in hands-on efforts tend to engage learners physically and emotionally in both the process of learning and the outcomes of the experience. This type of embodied learning is memorable exactly because it looks and feels different from what has come to be commonplace in education, learning through lecture or other passive means.

The power of such experiences can be traced to a simple idea: By being physically involved in an event that impels a learner to do the very thing he or she is learning about, multiple aspects of the person are engaged; thus the process feels genuine, and the outcomes are meaningful and personal. The wisdom of this learning methodology is not new; nor is the rationale for using it. In a saying that goes back to ancient China, the teacher (or perhaps it is meant for the student) is reminded "What I hear I forget, what I see I remember, what I do I understand." In other words, the physical experience is fundamental to learning that is truly implementable and transferable.

When utilized within a context of reflection, this process is commonly referred to at experiential education. Viewed within the theories of adult education, this methodology can fulfill what Boud, Keogh, and Walker (1985) note as being fundamentally important for such learners: "freeing them from habitual ways of thinking and acting" (p. 23). A direct, albeit backward, path can be drawn from this idea to Dewey's (1938) challenges of traditional educational methods, as illustrated in his questions: "How many [students] acquired special skills by means of automatic drill so that their power of judgment and capacity to act intelligently in new situations was limited? How many found what they did learn so foreign to the situations of life outside the school as to give them no power of control over the latter?" (p. 15). Both questions, while meant to illustrate Dewey's concern over the education of youth, can just as easily be asked of adult education, and with perhaps even more potency, since so many adult learners seek education to acquire learning that is immediately applicable in an array of situations.

Experiential Learning: Bringing the Physical into Learning

The process by which embodied experiences cross into learning that encompasses full understanding and thus has the potential to become education is perhaps most easily observed in the way children acquire skills, especially skills that relate to physical activities. As the father of a daughter who recently began riding a bicycle without training wheels, I saw that the physical and psychological aspects of learning how to make a two-wheel bike work are highlighted each time she attempts to head down the street on her bike. The embodied side of her learning is displayed in her experimentations with moving her body in different ways as she attempts to keep the bike in balance as she pedals. It is a seemingly straightforward task, and yet very quickly the psychological aspects of learning this skill come into play.

In my attempts to assist her, it has become clear that I can talk, demonstrate, tell, and plead with her all I want, yet the reality remains that learning this skill is going to happen only once she builds a certain level of comfort on her bike. Riding a bike is, after all, at least partially about confidence. The actions that go into riding a bike—pedaling, braking, balancing, looking forward—are physical, yet success is dependent on the mind-set of the person undertaking them. Because of this, my daughter, who is cautious in most things she does, has yet to truly be successful because her fears and concerns get in the way of the actions she needs to take.

Experiential Education and the Extension of the Embodied Experience

As embodied as the process of learning to ride a bicycle is, there is an undeniable connection between the physical and the mental, even if my daughter has not yet come to understand it this way. It does not take much observation to see that my daughter's most successful attempts coincide with those times when she is mentally confident and at ease enough to allow herself to physically relax. The reason for this is no great mystery. It is difficult to balance a bicycle when your body is tense, and of course it is hard to release physical tension when your mind is gripped with fear. Her fear comes from understanding that to fall while riding on pavement is going to hurt. This exacerbates her internal conflict between what she is mentally doing and what she physically needs to do: relax herself mentally and physically.

It is this dichotomy—the physical and mental being at odds with each other at those times when we are presented with a challenging experience—that gave rise to the educational methodology known as experiential education. By using the conflict between the physical and mental, it is believed that the potential to fulfill broad learning outcomes, such as increasing self-esteem, enhancing interpersonal relationships, and improving leadership capabilities, can be met. The trick, however, is finding a way to assist learners in drawing out of their experience those aspects that move beyond the purely physical and into these more ethereal aspects of learning that are implementable in other situations. So while in experiential education an embodied experience is fundamental to the learning process, it is being used primarily to create a setting in which learners are physically engaged but also mentally and socially challenged so that these challenges can be overcome, reflected on, and used as a basis for future actions.

Experiential Education as It Is Defined Today

Priest and Gass (1997) stated that adventure education, a subcategory of experiential education, involves a process in which the learner is placed into a unique physical and social environment, then given a set of problem-solving tasks that create a state of adaptive dissonance to which the learner adapts by mastery, which reorganizes the meaning and direction of the learner's experience.

Consider the unique physical experience had by an inexperienced individual climbing a mountain as part of a group made up of individuals originally unknown to the participant (a situation that provides for a unique social environment). The experience is had as part of a process of exploration that includes reflecting on the experience during and afterward, thereby reorganizing the meaning and direction of the individual's experience. The full spectrum of components of adventure education have been met in this scenario. How do these disparate parts come together? The answer to this is present in the history of experiential education.

Kurt Hahn and the Founding of Experiential Education

Kurt Hahn, a German educator who fled his country for England after being jailed by the Nazis for his outspoken opposition, became known in the 1930s and 1940s for his unique approach to education. Richards (1999) described this approach as addressing areas Hahn called declines in personal attributes in youth (and society): the decline of fitness, initiative, imagination, craftsmanship, self-discipline, and compassion. To address these, Hahn introduced a series of physical experiences for his students. His purpose and process for doing so is illustrated by his approach to enhancing "initiative." Hahn utilized expeditions to the mountains for his students so that they had adventurous experiences. In a speech, Hahn explained his purpose for doing so: "[Expeditions] revealed the inner worth of the man, the edge of his temper, the fiber of his stuff, the quality of resistance, the secret truth of his pretenses, not only to himself but to others" (quoted in Richards, 1999, p. 67). What is perhaps most significant in this quote is the lack of focus on the physical side of the experience despite the fact that the expeditions were intentionally physically difficult. Instead Hahn's attention was on the emotional, social, and psychological.

This process of utilizing physically difficult experiences to produce psychological growth came to be employed for a more specific purpose after Hahn was enlisted to develop a training regimen for young sailors early in World War II. As retold by Miner (1999), the owners of a merchant marine company asked Hahn to find a solution to a phenomenon among their sailors. Young sailors who initially survived torpedo attacks by the German military were dying during their ordeals aboard lifeboats, but not due to physical injuries. The theory was that the sailors were dying due to their lack of experience with overcoming the very challenging circumstances they faced once they were cast out to sea in a lifeboat. In essence, it was believed that the young sailors were simply giving up in the face of what they perceived as overwhelming conditions. Older sailors who had experience on sailing ships (as opposed to the engine propelled ships being used at the time) had a much greater ability to withstand the experience because they had acquired a sense of wind and weather, a reliance on their own resources, and a selfless bond with their fellow sailors. In response, Hahn created a monthlong training experience for the young sailors that combined small-boat experiences, athletics, rescue training, land and sea expeditions, and service. By combining these elements, Hahn was in fact developing what has come to be a template that continues in use today for teaching through physical experiences.

Current Practices in Experiential Education

Hahn created a basis for utilizing physical experiences to influence psychological outcomes, but current practices in experiential education commonly include an additional element. In their modeling of experiential education practices through time, Priest and Gass (1999) identified six generations of practices. Programs that offered organized wilderness experiences in the early 1900s were labeled "first generation" and identified as having had a process that largely let the experience speak for itself and thus allowed the experience to remain primarily in the physical realm. Priest and Gass (1999) noted that participants may "well have had a good time and possibly become proficient at new skills, but they were less likely to have learned anything about themselves, how they related with others, or how to resolve issues confronting them in their lives" (p. 216).

In contrast, third-generation facilitation, which is perhaps most widely practiced today, continues to rely on the physical experience as key to the learning process but makes use of reflection as a fundamental part of the overall experience. In adding this element, an environment for learners is created that emphasizes focusing on individual and group actions. Thus, the experience itself becomes less an end for and of itself. In practice, the use of reflection during an experience involves discussions that allow participants to review how they personally and as a group responded to a challenge, how they succeeded and where they fell short, how they reacted to failures, and how they plan to make use of their successes and failures during future challenges. The value of utilizing experiential education with adult learners can be seen most clearly during programming that includes the use of reflection; it is here that this learning methodology provides a means for taking education outside of the learning environment itself and into areas in which adult learners operate most: workplace, community, and family. As Kolb and Lewis (1986) stated, "Experiential learning encourages reflection on the meaning of abstract concepts as these concepts are highlighted through experiences and encouraging individual action through the act of committing to an idea and thus accepting responsibility for choosing that idea and for acquiring the knowledge to fully utilize the idea" (p. 100). In this way, adult learners are provided with an opportunity to transfer what they have experienced (learned) into other settings, a goal for most learners, for sure, but an aspect of learning that is especially important for adults.

Experiential Education in Practice

It is nearly impossible to list all of the ways that experiential education has been implemented since Hahn created his sailor-training program. Universities utilize it as part of freshman orientation programs to provide students with a shared experience; therapeutic practitioners use it as a means to address addictions by providing experiences that create a setting for incremental change; secondary schools use it as a way to curtail bullying by giving students a reason to work collaboratively; and businesses use it to engage their employees in making operations more efficient and profitable through effective teamwork.

Despite this variety, what these many practices look like in action is remarkably similar, whether the physical experience consists of a multiweek wilderness expedition or a single-day team-building and high-ropes course experience. In each situation, participants are presented with a set of incrementally difficult challenges to overcome and are given the tools to do so. During a wilderness trip, this may consist of learning how to pack a backpack, set up a tent, cook over a camp stove, and use a map and compass to navigate. During a team-building program, a group may be given a series of increasingly complex initiatives (problem-solving tasks) to complete. During each task, participants are being challenged (physically and mentally), which tends to create mental and social distress. Well managed, this distress creates opportunities to break down barriers and opens the potential for self-discovery by individuals and groups.

For example, while working at an organization that offered team-building programs (this term tends to mean many different things to people and thus we used it as a starting point to discovering a group's true goals—often these included building bonds between group members while also improving interpersonal communication skills, problem-solving skills, decision-making skills, goal-setting skills, or other similar group attributes), the editor of this volume was a client and brought her cohort group of doctoral students to my program early in their multiyear program. During a single-day experience, this group of middle-age individuals of various races, ethnicities, personal backgrounds, and physical capabilities was brought together and presented with group initiatives and a high-ropes course experience (a series of traversing elements built 35 feet off the ground). Her goals for the group consisted of creating an opportunity for the students to get to know each other, bond with one another, and explore their role within the group while simultaneously creating an opportunity for discussions about the impending challenges (academic and personal—balancing school, family, and work) they were undertaking.

As with any group, typically some members were hesitant to participate. These hesitations appeared to stem from a desire to avoid looking foolish, concerns about physical ability, and a hesitation to put the self in an unknown situation. To overcome these concerns, we were careful to choose activities and to present and reflect on them in ways that reassured the participants that they would have choices, a key attribute for successful adult programming. We also sought to build confidence within the group and individuals by slowly increasing the level of challenge (physically, socially, and emotionally) and stressing the need for the group to support one another. In this way, a shared experience was had that, upon examination, was parallel to the academic journey this group was undertaking.

For example, consider the activity called Helium Hoop, which consists of a group trying to raise a hula hoop that each group member is touching with one finger from the ground up to a set height without anyone losing contact. It is a seemingly simple but in practice very difficult challenge. At first glance it has practically nothing to do with obtaining a doctoral degree. On reflection afterward, however, the participants noted that while they disliked the activity because they struggled at it, they ultimately found it to be a great learning experience because it illustrated to them the natural role that each person took within the group. During a time of stress, group members fell back into the natural roles that each felt most comfortable with. Left to develop on its own during their academic classes, this process of discovering the true attributes of their fellow classmates undoubtedly would have taken far longer than the 25 minutes of this activity. This was a small but important step if the group members were to truly get to know one another.

This group also participated in our high-ropes course, a significant challenge for some because it called on them to climb to a height of 35 feet, then to traverse elements built out of ropes and metal cables and finally to exit the course via a zip line. A zip line is attached to a pulley that, in turn, is attached to a person's harness and a metal cable that traverses from a point on a high-ropes course to or near the ground. Again, fears of physical ability, of looking foolish in front of colleagues, and others surfaced along with fears about being off the ground. Working with such concerns is very much the purpose of challenging the group members to climb up and through the ropes course: to elicit a sense of being challenged in multiple ways. Success, therefore, carries multiple levels of accomplishment and feels genuine because participants have chosen to take on the challenge and break through physical and mental barriers to do so.

With this group, the use of the ropes course complemented challenges members had experienced earlier. But with the ropes course, a more personal challenge was faced while bonds built between group members earlier could be enhanced through the process of having individuals within the group emotionally support each other. Thus, a challenge that was very physically and mentally real for participants and that elicited efforts to support one another but had no outward connection to the classroom was, in fact, again creating the conditions necessary for group success in the classroom: a willingness to take on challenges, empathy among cohort members, a desire to assist one another, and personal feelings of accomplishment. It is difficult, after all, to be part of a shared experience that includes experiencing or seeing others go through moments of great trepidation, face their fears, and overcome them without feeling that you know that person more fully.

Instances of individuals arriving at the platform where the zip line originated only to be gripped by uncertainty occurred with this and most groups that came to the course. In part, this was a manifestation of the realization that often occurred to participants once they were attached to the zip-line element. They alone were going to be responsible for taking the final step off of the platform and into thin air. Fundamental to our process at the course was a strict refusal to "assist" anyone off the platform by pushing or otherwise getting a person to take the step that would move him or her away from the platform via the zip line. While many requested such assistance and even insisted that it was the only way they would move, doing so would have undercut a key aspect of the experience: creating a setting where participants were fully responsible for their actions and thus could own their accomplishments. This routinely meant extended waits at the zip-line platform filled with discussion, calm reassurance, and support, but the final result was all the better for it.

However, if this embodied experience, as real and powerful for the participants as it was, was simply completed and then left as a stand-alone occurrence without reflection or discussion, it would likely have been a time of fond memories that jump-started the development of relationships between students but not much more. As Boud, Keogh, and Walker stated (1985), "If we are exposed to one new event after another without a break we are unlikely to be able to make the most of any of the events separately" (p. 26).

Reflective Learning from Experiential Education

To increase learning from embodied experiences, third-generation programs utilize reflection tools. A simple example of one such tool consists of a set of three questioning words and phrases: What? So what? Now what? These three questions can be used to assist a group through an impasse or elicit group members to discuss their experience and thereby fulfill what Boud, Keogh, and Walker (1985) referred to as "stages of reflection, Returning to the experience, Attending to feelings and Re-evaluating the experience" (p. 26).

The "What?" question asks the group to list everything that occurred during a specific period or experience: actions taken, group planning or lack thereof, goal setting, and group communication. The "So what?" question builds off these responses and pushes group members to qualify their individual actions and the actions of the group. Responses to the "So what?" question get the group focused on aspects of their actions such as the quality of interactions between group members (supportive, argumentative, divisive), which can be instructive in revealing group members' feelings for one another and other social, emotional, and intellectual aspects occurring within the group. Through this question, group members are able to see for themselves how they are functioning.

Finally, the "Now what?" question is asked, and group members are encouraged to apply insights developed thus far to overcome the challenges that have been presented or that they will face later by making a plan of action. Here, for example, a group that has been unsuccessfully trying the same solution to a problem-solving initiative over and over again will begin to determine why this is occurring and to make a plan to overcome this barrier to success. It is also at this point that group members begin to look toward how their actions and interactions might transfer to other aspects of their lives.

Ultimately, through this set of debriefing questions, group members can gain great insight into the actions and behaviors of individuals and groups.

Extensive personal and social understanding can result from a physical experience involving activities that are seemingly irrelevant to everyday life. Kurt Hahn sought to provide young sailors with the mental fortitude to survive long enough to be rescued by giving them an experience that was not simply of the sea but through the sea (Miner, 1999) and, thus, was broad enough to build their capacity to overcome tremendous psychological distress. So too can the lessons learned through direct experiences be transferred to areas of life that extend well beyond the defined experience itself.

References

Boud, D., Keogh, R., and Walker, D. *Reflection: Turning Experience into Learning.* New York: Nichols Publishing, 1985.

Dewey, J. *Experience and Education.* New York: Macmillan, 1938.

Kolb, D., and Lewis, L. *Experiential and Simulation Techniques for Teaching Adults.* New Directions for Continuing Education, no.30. San Francisco: Jossey-Bass, 1986.

Miner, J. "The Creation of Outward Bound." In John C. Miles and Simon Priest (eds.), *Adventure Programming.* State College, Pa.: Venture Publishing, 1999.

Priest, S., and Gass, M. *Effective Leadership in Adventure Programming.* Champaign, Ill.: Human Kinetics, 1997.

Priest, S., and Gass, M. "Six Generations of Facilitation Skills." In John C. Miles and Simon Priest (eds.), *Adventure Programming.* State College, Pa.: Venture Publishing, 1999.

Richards, A. "Kurt Hahn." In John C. Miles and Simon Priest (eds.), *Adventure Programming.* State College, Pa.: Venture Publishing, 1999.

ERIC HOWDEN *is director of operations for Global Youth Leadership Institute in Milwaukee, Wisconsin.*

This article explores dance as a way of knowing, inquiry, embodied understanding and, ultimately, what it can mean to think on our feet and get our feet in our thinking.

Dance as a Way of Knowing

Celeste Snowber

Dance as a Birthright

Dance is our birthright. Movement is knitted into the fabric of our beings, and the very first dance begins in the womb. No one who has had a child in the womb can deny that the first signs of life are the movements and kicks of the child within. We become creatures of extended palms and open chests, contractions and extensions, skips and falls, clenched fists and swaying hips. As children we have what I call a body signature, a dance of our own. Delight is taken in the wind sweeping through limbs, and exhilaration is found in hopping, jumping, dancing on the beach, or just skipping down the street. Uninhibited joy is the mark on the flesh. Until we were habituated otherwise, learning in school was associated with "paying attention," which was equated with sitting still rather than being deeply engaged.

For example, when one of my sons would be twirling and moving in the kitchen, I would say to him "Listen to me," as if he couldn't twirl and listen. And he would say to me, so astutely "Perhaps you can't multitask anymore, Mom, but I can." In movement he could inhabit a still mind. I resonate with this as a dancer, a walker, and a swimmer. In movement my mind slows down enough to truly listen—listen to the bold proclamations and the gentle whispers; the ones within and the whispers without.

This article invites the reader to consider dance as a way of knowing. It extends dance to include not only the more formal way one thinks of dance but creative movement, improvisation, and ways of moving that are marked by expressivity. This is particularly important in postsecondary educational settings, where there are a wide variety of backgrounds brought by students through diverse experiences. One cannot take only one class or a semester, and refine the skills to teach or learn dance in all of its rich forms. It is a lifetime of practice and artistry, not to mention muscular and physical requirements to become adept at any particular discipline. Kinesthetic knowing is central to being human, and the beginning of dance is found in the wide expression of gestural language. While one can lie with one's lips, it is almost impossible to lie with the body. The body is a place of deep knowing, as Martha Graham, the pioneer modern dancer, so beautifully said many years ago: "Movement never lies. It is a barometer telling the state of the soul's weather to all who can read it" (1991, p. 4).

Embodied Knowing

Cases have been made over and over again for the importance of embodied learning and the connection of mind and body and the importance of somatic learning (Bresler, 2004; Cancienne, 2008; Cancienne and Megibow, 2001; Richmond and Snowber, 2009). I come to this work from various disciplines including arts education, spiritual theology, and poetics, but most significantly my work on dance education draws on my theoretical foundation in curriculum theory (Blumenfeld-Jones, 1995; Malewski, 2009; Pinar, 1994) and the practice of Interplay (Winton-Henry and Porter, 1997, 2004) and my background in dance as embodied prayer (Snowber, 2004).

In this short article, I would like to call to attention the significance of how dance can be a place of inquiry and its generative possibilities for deeper understanding. I have been engaging in a practice with both my students and myself for decades, integrating dance as a way of asking the questions. We dance the questions, we write the questions, and we go back and forth from our limbs and torsos to finding breath in our words on the page. Sensuous knowledge is our map for the journey. We know what we know, but I am curious about what it is we don't know. How can we be surprised and catapulted into fresh insight and ripe knowing? The paradigm of knowledge in Western culture has been primarily education as an accumulation of knowledge. This volume centers on knowledge as embodied, and I would suggest that embodied knowing is a knowing that we need to desperately recover for the health of the planet.

Dance as a way of knowing investigates dance as a form "beyond the steps" yet includes steps. These steps are not so much left and right, back and forth, stage center, but the steps of recovering a visceral language that has the capacity to connect body, mind, heart, soul, and imaginative thinking. I have spent a lifetime integrating dance and movement within undergraduate and graduate education in a variety of educational programs as a means to access our body knowledge. The context of my teaching is preservice teachers and graduate students in arts education, health education, and ecological education. My passion is to find ways to connect writing from the body, where the words dance, and we can dance our words, and ultimately the body is let out, opening a way for a way of theorizing through flesh. Connecting to bodily knowledge could be likened to having a free GPS system within us, always available to guide, and dance breaks open the boundaries for listening with all our beings (Snowber, 2011). In other words, we need our full bodies for deeper understanding of what it means to be human in this world.

Dance and the Lived Body

Dance in its many forms has the capacity to invite us into what it means to be uninhibited in our bodies, to think through movement. Maxine Sheets-Johnstone (1999), who is well known for writing on phenomenology and movement, says, "Thinking in movement is foundational to being a body" (p. 494). Dance invites us to think on our feet and get our feet in our thinking. I have been working with student teachers for many years, and I tell them over and over again, as Parker Palmer (1998) says, "We teach who we are" (p. 2), yet part of who we are is an embodied people. As soon as we walk across the classroom, the students know if the teacher feels confident in relating to the class. We teach with and through our bodies. I call it body pedagogy (Snowber, 2005), and integrate movement as a way for students to make friends with their bodies. We do not have bodies; we *are* bodies. However, one cannot live in Western culture and not take the impact of cultural constructs that emphasize what we look like instead of how we experience sensations through our bodies. It is clear that body knowledge has become endangered within the human species, and we are often alienated in our own bodies. The emphasis has been on the outer body as opposed to what I would call, in more phenomenological terms, "the lived body." The lived body is the felt body where we make connections to the multiple sensations around and within us. The feel of the wind on the skin, fingers typing at the computer, the pain in the lower back, the joy of one torso swimming, and the tears in the belly all connect us to the lived body. We are creatures of turns and twists, contractions and expanse, gestures and postures, although it feels as if Western culture has forgotten we have hips. I tell my students that they are in the only class where they must learn pelvic inquiry, to loosen their hips and bellies for that matter, and know, as many other cultures do, that there is knowledge in those forbidden realms of the body. We came from the belly and hips and we must return there. This isn't knowledge that can just be told or read about; it must be experienced. And in experiencing, there is as much unlearning to do as learning.

The Play of Dance—the Dance of Play

Spinning and dancing, which were once so organic to us as children, have often been lost in adulthood. I often instruct give my undergraduate movement education students a first assignment to go watch children on the playground and even get on the swings themselves because doing so is to be deeply alive in their bodies. The movements of play on the playground can elicit the body memory of what it was like to feel the gestures of hopping, skipping, throwing, swinging, hanging, and stomping—everyday gestures of the playground. I have my students write and reflect out of their movement experiences because the components of play, risk, creativity, and improvisation elicit both a language of movement and the language of the heart (Snowber, 1997).

Movement has the capacity to touch us physically and emotionally at our roots, provoking the deepest emotions, from love to fear to joy to abandon. One of the central aspects of dance that I integrate in my own work with students is the act of play. Dance has the capacity to be the muscle of the imagination, a magical invitation through the creative process to reimagine new worlds. This is the same imagination that is needed for every new beginning in life, whether it is a different way to lead, a personal decision, a cure for cancer, or a way to build the bones of innovation. The art of play connects each of us to material that is often dormant in our lives, whether that is a new way of moving, accessing places of emotion, or inspiration. The creativity of dance accesses the place within us that has primal imagination. Integrating play within dance making has the capacity to return us to the place where we lose inhibitions of the self-consciousness of our bodies and re-member our bodies back to themselves (Snowber, 2007). Play also gives us the courage to access aspects of dance making, which include lament and sorrow, for the paradox of both beauty and loss always honors the whole person's experience in the world.

Dance and Literacy

No matter what we are teaching, when the curriculum is embodied we come to a deeper understanding of concepts, ideas, or new ways of thinking. Research continues to connect the relationship between dance and the embodied brain and interrelate the importance of brain function and movement (Mason, 2009). Dance can be integrated into all aspects of the curriculum, and dance has connected to all aspects of the curriculum from kindergarten through grade twelve (Hanna, 2008). Dance is needed as we recover what it means to be adults in the world, learning with mind, body, and soul. We can dance our stories, understand the nuances of Shakespeare or Neruda, or dissect cultural constructs when they are released in the body. My experience with adult learners is that if they have an opportunity to move the ideas they are grappling with into their bodies, they have the capacity to come to new ways of understanding. The expressivity of movement allows for images to take flesh and, ultimately, new perceptions to develop. Movement and dance are not just ways to illustrate ideas but a way of grappling more deeply with the complexity of ways students can critically think, sift, perceive, and eventually come to fresh understanding of whatever subject they are studying. Dance is an invitation to think with our entire beings. It ushers in a way to connect biology and body, economics and intuitive thinking, human geography and physicality, and psychology and visceral awareness.

Dance as a Way of Inquiry

How do we know what we know? Why do we think that it is only the mind that can unravel and discover knowledge when it is often our senses—the smell of lilacs, which remind us of childhood, or the feeling of swaying back and forth, which exudes comfort? We are an embodied people, designed as our birthright to dance and move. Dance accesses many kinds of knowledge beyond kinesthetic intelligence, including visual, tactile, mental, cognitive, and emotional intelligence. And the contribution of dance, choreography, and improvisation to a broad way of understanding and perception is clear from the works of dance education scholars over the years (Fraleigh, 2004; Hanna, 1987, 2008; Shapiro, 1999; Stinson, 1995).

How are questions changed when we ask them through our bodies? When I access a question through dance, I evoke words, thought, and uncoverings that go beyond the tricks my mind can pull. How does the body connect to what is happening in the ecological sphere? How can dance reveal global warming or what is happening to the planet? The curriculum of our lives has the capacity to become the canvas from which is drawn upon as a place where theory has the opportunity to be enfleshed into practice. Accessing this canvas is much more possible when the language of dance can touch to the roots of experience and knowing. The body has constant data that speaks to us, whether it is the flurry in the stomach, the stretch of an elbow, or the abrupt contraction. Body data is the information that occurs in the present moment, the immediate present time, the ways we experience information through our bodies (Winton-Henry and Porter, 1997). The choreographer and performer have long known that the creative process is one of questioning and sifting, forming and unforming, making and remaking, and always a place of discovery (Cancienne, 2008; Cancienne and Snowber, 2003). By dancing our questions, we can uncover the questions underneath the questions and open up a deep listening to the body's knowledge. Dance awakens us to emotional and spiritual intelligence, as Anna Halprin (2000), a pioneer in integrating dance as a place of discovery, has modeled for many years. The dancer follows the movement impulse and is awakened to the nuances of the language of the heart, one that calls us back to an ancient way of knowing. The place of not knowing is fertile ground for excavating the choreographic process and opening the whole body and mind to a place of growth. Knowledge opens to the dancer in ways that are particular to the body's insight through its capacity to explore both balance and nonbalance, gravity and levity, or contraction and release. Principles of composition in dance and improvisation have correlations to how one can perceive and understand themselves and the world around them.

Central to this creative process to which I am speaking is the art of improvisation, the necessary ingredient for all creativity. A movement and writing exercise that I integrate with adult learners is to open up the places to not only dance the questions but to write out of the experience of dancing. Dance opens up to our breath, the tongue of language that is rooted in our bodies. When we write from our sweat, our words uncover knowing that we did not know. I ask students to do a free write after dancing from these few words: "My body knows. . . ." The jewels that break forth are always amazing, and how much body wisdom is within each one.

Our lives are a dance in progress, as we are informed, formed, and transformed in the rich palette of lived experience. Dance is the invitation to reclaim an embodied inspiration—the entrance to our knowing that is filled with a lifetime of mystery and magic. More than ever, it is the questions that we must pay attention to, dance from, and live into a new way of being in the world. As we dance into the unknown and the known, we can birth the breath of new words.

The Body Knows
Dance is a way to break
spill, turn, twist and extend
the knowing of the cells
juicy and jagged
an ancient space
where the feet think
and the belly listens
the sternum proclaims and
the kidneys lament

The body longs to be present
and be with presence
let out of the classrooms, offices and homes
and dance its way back to wonder
take each form as multiple celebrations
and bring the body home
to its rightful place
where we honor
the footnotes of our bodies

Dance your questions—
what you know and don't know

and know this:
what is within you
is fluttering, seeking a form
so loosen your joints
awaken your muscles
and breathe into your limbs
and dance your way
into new steps.

This article has sought to expand the ways that movement and dance can be thought about and practiced in connection to adult learning. Ultimately, dance is a way for adults to be opened up to embodied learning and not only connect to themselves with their bodies, minds, heart, and imagination but to more deeply understand and question the world around them. The most significant value dance brings is to invite learners into a different relationship with their bodies. This can relate to a variety of content areas in a curriculum as it shifts the curriculum of their own bodies. When we inhabit our bodies fully, no matter what vocation is in our lives, we are able to integrate the fullness of our intelligence, incorporating the emotional, kinesthetic, conceptual, and our complete humanity. We are fully alive, vibrating under our skin, and live with presence. This is a presence of knowing and experiencing our full vitality. And in this place we encounter the deep wisdom of our bodies, what we came into the world with, and what we need more than ever in this day and age. Dance opens us up so we can show up for our own lives and once again fall into wonder.

References

Blumenfeld-Jones, D. "Dance as a Mode of Research Representation." *Qualitative Inquiry*, 1995, *1*(4) 391–401.

Bresler, L. (ed.). *Knowing Bodies, Moving Minds: Towards Embodied Teaching and Learning.* Dordrecht, the Netherlands: Kluwer, 2004.

Cancienne, M. B. "From Research Analysis to Performance: The Choreographic Process." In J. G. Knowles and A. Cole (eds.), *The Handbook of the Arts in Qualitative Research: Perspectives, Methodologies, Examples, and Issues.* New York: Sage, 2008.

Cancienne, M. B., and Megibow, A. "The Story of Anne: Movement as Educative Text." *Journal of Curriculum Theorizing*, 2001, *17*(2), 61–72.

Cancienne, M. B., and Snowber, C. "Writing Rhythm: Movement as Method." *Qualitative Inquiry*, 2003, *9*(2), 237–253.

Fraleigh, S. *Dancing Identity: Metaphysics in Motion.* Pittsburg, PA: University of Pittsburg Press, 2004.

Graham, M. *Blood Memory.* New York: Doubleday, 1991.

Halprin, A. *Dance as a Healing Art: Returning to Health with Movement and Imagery.* Mendocino, Calif.: LifeRhythm, 2000.

Hanna, J. L. *To Dance Is Human: A Theory of Nonverbal Communication* (rev. ed.). Chicago: University of Chicago Press, 1987.

Hanna, J. L. "A Nonverbal Language for Imagining and Learning: Dance Education in K–12 Curriculum." *Educational Researcher*, 2008, 37(8) 491–506.

Malewski, E. (ed.). *Curriculum Studies Handbook: The Next Moment, Exploring Post-Reconceptualization.* New York: Routledge, 2009.

Mason, P. H. "Brain, Dance and Culture: The Choreographer, the Dancing Scientist and Interdisciplinary Collaboration—Broad Hypotheses of an Intuitive Science of Dance." *Brolga: An Australian Journal about Dance*, 2009, 30, 27–34.

Palmer, P. J. *The Courage to Teach: Exploring the Inner Landscape of a Teacher's Life.* San Francisco: Jossey-Bass, 1998.

Pinar, W. *Autobiography, Politics, and Sexuality: Essays in Curriculum Theory 1972–1992.* New York: Peter Lang, 1994.

Richmond, S., and Snowber, C. *Landscapes in Aesthetic Education.* Newcastle upon Tyne, United Kingdom: Cambridge Scholars, 2009.

Shapiro, S. (ed.). *Dance, Power, and Difference: Critical Feminist Perspectives on Dance Education.* Champaign, Ill.: Human Kinetics International, 1999.

Sheets-Johnstone, M. *The Primacy of Movement.* Philadelphia: John Benjamin, 1999.

Snowber, C. "Writing the Body." *Educational Insights*, 1997, 4(1). http://www.educationalinsights.ca/.

Snowber, C. *Embodied Prayer: Towards Wholeness of Body Mind Soul.* Kelowna, Canada: Northstone, 2004.

Snowber, C. "The Eros of Teaching." In J. Miller and others (eds.), *Holistic Learning and Spirituality in Education: Breaking New Ground.* Albany: State University of New York, 2005.

Snowber, C. "The Soul Moves: Dance and Spirituality in Educative Practice." In L. Bresler (ed.), *International Handbook for Research in the Arts and Education.* Dordrecht, the Netherlands: Springer, 2007.

Snowber, C. "Let the Body Out: A Love Letter to the Academy from the Body." In E. Malewski and N. Jaramillo (eds.), *Epistemologies of Ignorance in Education.* Charlotte, N.C.: Information Age, 2011.

Stinson, S. "Body of Knowledge." *Educational Theory*, 1995, 45(1), 43–54.

Winton-Henry, C., and Porter, P. *Having It All: Body, Mind, Heart and Spirit Together Again at Last.* Oakland, Calif.: Wing It! Press, 1997.

Winton-Henry, C., and Porter, P. *What the Body Wants.* Kelowna, Canada: Northstone, 2004.

CELESTE SNOWBER, Ph.D., is a dancer, writer, educator, and associate professor in the Faculty of Education at Simon Fraser University outside Vancouver, British Columbia. She specializes in dance and arts education; has written extensively in the area of the arts, embodiment, and education; and continues to perform her dance and poetry in a variety of settings.

This article explores how somatic theater processes tap into embodied knowing, which enables and animates participants to see themselves as creators of their own stories, knowledge, and actions for justice.

Embodied Knowledge and Decolonization: Walking with Theater's Powerful and Risky Pedagogy

Shauna Butterwick, Jan Selman

SHAUNA: In a course I was teaching with elementary teacher education students, we talked about their practice experience and how teachers are in the public eye "performing" a professional image. We read a script that focused on how teachers were always being watched (Hurren, Moskal, and Wasylowich 2001). Three students volunteered to perform the dialogue, including one man who played the role of the female teacher. In the beginning there was much laughter, and I encouraged them to treat all the characters with care and respect. The class grew quieter and more serious. After the reading, we continued to talk about the audiences who were watching them and interpreting their actions, and I directed them to link this discussion to our ongoing exploration of how sexism, racism, classism, and homophobia are operating in the education system and, in particular, how teachers perform and how they are judged by others. This time they got it at a deeper level.

Theater processes can powerfully connect mind, body, and emotions, providing opportunities and spaces for transformation. Based in stories from our disparate but complementary practices, we focus here on facilitators' ethical responsibilities when bringing theater activities to processes of critical deconstruction of oppressive relations. While encouraging the use of theater and embodied pedagogy, pointing to its transformational power, we emphasize that taking on these issues involves a set of decisions and responsibilities. Our reflections are informed by somatic theories of theater critics and practitioners, feminist discussions of the importance of reclamation of individual and communal body, memory and story, and critical pedagogy, including decolonizing and transformative pedagogies. We aim to discuss not merely how theater and embodied activities contribute to a remembering and naming of oppression but also how these processes may be facilitated in such a way as to generate new knowledge that leads to enfranchisement and action.

Working in these transformative spaces can be risky, even harmful. While embodied theater processes can reveal meaningful stories that create opportunities for building community and commonalities, reflection, analysis, and strategizing for action, they can trigger unremembered and unprocessed stories and memories. The potential for surprise and danger needs be recognized and anticipated, to avoid overwhelming individuals, groups, or facilitators. The power of embodied learning should not be underestimated; these experiences must be embraced and turned to positive outcomes.

Defining the Territory

Those who write about popular theater or related approaches, including drama and theater for development, transformational theater, applied theater, and others, work toward a succinct definition (see Jackson, 2007; Kidd, 1979; Prentki and Selman, 2000). *Popular theater* implies theater and theater processes used in the service of communities, to uncover, define, and work toward social change. A key element is community participation, and the goal is transformative action for greater equity and justice. We are particularly interested in how theater processes seek to make explicit oppressive practices that, we argue, are a form of violence. Young (1990) pointed to how violence operates at a relational and psychic level, "depriving the oppressed of freedom and dignity" (p. 62). Furthermore she highlights the social dimension of violence: "everyone knows it happens and will happen again . . . always at the horizon of social imagination" (p. 62).

The embodied processes of theater offer great potential to interrupt such forms of violence and to contribute to decolonization. As Tejedes and Espinoza (2003) argued, decolonization assumes an understanding that the neocolonialism that exists in the United States—and, we would argue, Canada—"has its origins in the mutually reinforcing systems of colonial and capitalist domination and exploitation" (p. 11). A decolonizing pedagogy thus "insists that colonial domination and its ideological frameworks operate and are reproduced in and through the design of community and education-based practice" (Tejedes and Espinoza, pp. 20–21). Theater provides avenues for decolonizing oppressive gender politics and deepening understandings of gender as a performance. As Judith Butler (2004) argued, if the performance of gender "is mistaken for a natural or linguistic given, power is relinquished to expand the cultural field bodily through subversive performances of various kinds" (p. 164).

Many authors, including Asher (2005), explicate how "the colonized/oppressed internalize the ways and language of the colonizer/oppressor, in order to survive within extant social structures" and how "decolonization and social transformation . . . are necessarily self-reflexive processes, requiring the deconstruction of not only the colonizer and external oppressive structures, but also one's own internalization of and participation in the same" (p. 1080). We try to subscribe to Asher's practice and to Masschelein's (2010) call for a process of "e-ducating the gaze" through forms of inquiry that lead to attentiveness. "Attention is the state of mind . . . which opens up to the world in such a way that the world can present itself to me (that I can 'come' to see) and I can be transformed" (p. 44).

In this spirit of self-reflexivity and attentiveness, we offer several stories from our practice.

Embodied Knowing and Decolonization

JAN: For me, until I spoke in depth one day with Darrell Wildcat, embodied knowing was about enfranchising my full self—body, emotion, spirit, as well as mind. Darrell, sadly no longer with us, was well known to many in the popular theater movement. He codeveloped a significant community play linking Aboriginal oral history and descendants of European prairie settlers and participated in some of the most significant international popular theater workshop encounters, hosting one of these events as part of our Canadian Popular Theatre Alliance Festival at his home reserve, Hobbema, Alberta. I went into theater because of personal, unifying, and holistic experiences. It challenged me and connected mind and body. But one day, many years later, I interviewed popular theater practitioners Jane Heather and Darrell Wildcat. I started to understand, beyond intellectual appreciation, some depths of the need for decolonization and the role somatic experiences can play in this difficult process. This is part of what Darrell said:

> I look at body a lot. The sexual abuse of people is really high, eh, some people say incidences of up to 75% of all Indian people have been abused. . . . For the longest time I never wanted to talk about what happened to me, eh, but it happened to me too. And then . . . all that is to me a colonial experience, so theatre becomes a decolonizing experience that brings people back together. Because you can't do theatre unless you use your body. And you can't express from your body unless you know how to do it. I always say that to people on the reserve. Every time you do theatre you are decolonizing people. 'Cause every time you are breaking that separation between body and self, reconnecting it back. And so maybe it's naive, but I think my community is so defined. (quoted in Prentki and Selman, 2000, p. 21)

When Darrell spoke these words, I felt he linked the body connecting experiences, which I recognized on a personal level, to something political. It was an aha moment, a step toward more richly realizing links between the personal and fierce, political implications that theater can encompass.

There is much here that speaks to Aboriginal people's experiences and to women whose bodies have been colonized. Processes of colonization can separate mind and body—that separation allows (is necessary) for domination and manipulation. However, separation is never complete; there is always a thread of connection that remains. Because, as Helen Nicholson suggests, "the aesthetic is a discourse on the body" (2005, p. 57), perhaps through participating in theater experiences the muted mind becomes embodied and sometimes the body finds voice, or perhaps the separate mind finally becomes the audience to the embodied intelligence.

JAN: I recall regularly encountering a challenging position during the '80s, when the popular theater movement was growing in leaps and bounds, worldwide. As many searched for how to best use this powerful tool, work such as the activities Darrell described was dismissed as primarily individualistic, apolitical, naive, bourgeois, or of little value in the search for social and political change. It was "personal development" rather than radically transformative. I recall finding the words I needed only after one of these encounters:

> In communities where leadership is scarce, where voice is disempowered, where social and personal lives are in much disarray, the journey is long. It needs to start where it can start, with a step, not a leap into a prescribed political action—if that is not timely. Drama for personal expression is one starting point; for some, standing up in front of peers and community and expressing a story or experience that rings true is a remarkable, huge step towards a sense that one matters and has agency. Other steps can follow.

Director Lina de Guevara defines this work as about both individual and social change in *Creating Bridges*, a video documentary about a community theater process, *I Wasn't Born Here: Stories of Latin American Immigrant Women*. She emphasizes physical work within theater making, including yoga, "because it teaches you where your limits are and you just keep pushing at those limits so you expand more and more" (Joy and Hood, 1988). Participant Yolanda Huerta speaks to a yoga-triggered experience:

> Doing this exercise I suddenly felt like fainting. Dizzy. I have this strange pain in my back, right down on the end point where there is a little bone. And then, I remember, when I was in the stadium, a military man kicked me back there. He kicked me with his boot. It was a horrible feeling. (Joy and Hood, 1988)

Unremembered memories are held in the body. Facilitators must ask groups to enter these areas with sensitivity. Gay Meagley, the project's yoga instructor, models one way to support the group while they explore somatically:

> All of us have emotions and thoughts that we store inside the body. So sometimes when you are working deeply like this, . . . these feelings . . . can suddenly surface. So don't be alarmed, don't be concerned if this happens. Sometimes we experience tremendous joy. Sometimes we experience sadness. So whatever the emotion is, allow it to percolate, to surface and to express itself. (Joy and Hood, 1988)

de Guevara declares:

> I really don't think you can work in art very well by using your reason. You have to use your intuition and your inspiration. You transform yourself. You become somebody that can express yourself but without realizing that you are doing it. So that you completely bypass all the intellectual thing, all the rationality. (Joy and Hood, 1988)

We don't agree with this fully. Although there is a stage where the mind can get in the way of deep experience and where processes should downgrade the dominance of the intellect, once the kinds of discoveries that are possible through somatic work occur, we have a chance to *integrate* feeling, body, and intellect. That makes a discovery memorable, deeply known, felt, reflected on, and therefore relevant.

Witnessing and Embodiment

SHAUNA: I often use theater exercises in teacher education and graduate courses. In one class I asked students to work in small groups and discuss whose interests were being served in relation to examples of adult learning from their own practice as adult educators. Discussions took longer than planned. I had hoped there would be time for groups to create tableaus or images that captured their dialogue. Improvising, I decided to illustrate, using myself as intelligent clay, an activity that involves molding bodies into different positions depicting relationships, notions, or attitudes. Standing at the front of the class, I invited a student familiar with these processes to shape me as the class called out words that had been part of their discussions.
We had a few minutes to debrief. Several students commented they enjoyed the process; it was not something they had seen before. They remarked how it helped to visualize elements of their discussion. Some were happy that I had not asked them to do this activity as it would have been uncomfortable for them. Then students had 10 minutes to write their reflections, which were handed in (something we did at the end of every class). One student wrote how she saw the sculpting

process as a kind of manipulation that made her reflect on the ethics of employee workshops she had run. I checked in with her next class, and she indicated she felt destabilized as her view of her practice had significantly changed. She found this both unnerving and exciting.

This story speaks to how an embodied activity can trigger a strong emotion, accompanied by a shift in thinking for its witnesses; audiences to theater processes are participants of the activities, not passive recipients. The "implicated audience" is something we've written about elsewhere (Butterwick and Selman, 2003). The student who witnessed the body-sculpting process perhaps tapped into some unconscious thinking about her practice. Julie Salverson (1996) spoke insightfully on the process of witnessing and "taking things personally." Such forms of engagement "enable a transformation of the listener's understanding of her or himself" (Salverson, p. 183).

This student's encounter could be viewed as perspective transformation, a shift in habits of mind and perspective as outlined by Jack Mezirow (1997), who calls on adult educators to create ideal conditions for these changes. An important aspect of this kind of shift is that it's felt in the body, often before intellectual interpretation. As Nicholson (2005) noted: "The body is a discursive category, a site of struggle. . . . Pedagogies which are embodied . . . involve a more complex understanding of how the body is culturally and socially constructed and experienced" (p. 59).

In the preceding event, it was important to provide a container to hold participants' sensations, like the debriefing, but public discussions have limitations. Individual reflective memos offered an additional space for going deeper. If there had been no opportunity to stay with the experience, if the class had ended right after the "clay" activity, some of this kind of knowing may not have been tapped.

The Safety and Power of Fiction

In addition to theater's engagement of the body, objects (and our physical relationship to them) can trigger powerful responses and reveal memories and stories with a jolt of recognition. Story sharing circles are a staple of popular theater. Story leads to meaning, with remembered events layering self-knowledge and knowledge of others. Freire (1983) proposed that the coding of our experiences (through community photos or, in the case of drama, through telling our stories) creates conditions where reality can be examined, assessed, and understood. The decodification process, discovering meanings, power structures, and social conditions within that world, can follow.

For the facilitator, the power of triggering story holds particular responsibilities. We can't know what may be unearthed. Attention is required. Masschelein (2010), referencing Foucault, argues: "In this kind of research knowledge is not meant for [improving our] understanding, but for 'cutting,' for concrete [bodily] inscription, and for transformation of who we are and how we live" (p. 47). While kinesthetic approaches are attractive, we are responsible for creating situations where the risk is mitigated by the group's commitments to one another, where the discovery of deep story through the body is honored, recognized, and given meaning.

One response to the need for attentive, responsible, and responsive leadership is to ask groups to create fictitious stories "that could be real." Group-created stories can provide protective distance for participants engaging in substantive exploration. "Snapshot stories" is a somatic exercise in which groups create and perform a story in a series of frozen pictures. Sometimes parameters are added; for example, a facilitator may propose that a story focus on a character "who could be a member of this group" and that it conclude with the last image "leaving her in a dilemma" (Selman, 1986, p. 23). But even through this more measured exercise, uncharted truths can surface.

JAN: To explore potential intervention points in community issues, a feminist artist group was making snapshot stories about crises in women's lives. Small groups worked physically and verbally to create these stories. As facilitator, I was taking a breath before circulating among five working groups. Suddenly a woman ran out of the room. Suddenly she was gone. I didn't see it happen.

The story the group created involved someone in an abusive home. As they built the snapshots, a fictitious story expressed physically, the experience was too much for one participant to handle. She escaped. "The first concern of this research is to be attentive" (Masschelein, 2010, p.47). An action-oriented workshop gave way to finding the colleague and ensuring her well-being. While this seemed to take us to a place different from the starting goals of the workshop, this occurrence was transformative.

JAN: We, the group and myself, learned more than if it had not happened. Emotion, spawned of physicalizing story, catapulted us into the value, urgency, and meaning of the work, and moved us to a new level of intensity. The need for action was more palpable. The need for attention and care-full approaches to the work called out. This transformative experience came from linking self, story, body, memory, and commitment.

There is often fear and resistance to the expression of strong emotions. When they arise they need attention. As Jagger (1992) argued, they can be significant sources of knowing: "Accepting the indispensability of appropriate emotions to knowledge means no more and no less than that the discordant emotions should be attended to seriously and respectfully rather than condemned, ignored, discounted, or suppressed" (p. 163).

JAN: As I recall this event and its implications, I wish I could go back now and learn about this woman's subsequent journey. What is her memory and meaning of that day?

Implications for Adult Educators

Embodied theater processes need pedagogical and ethical frames or containers so fear and other triggered emotions can be explored in such a way that participants are not stuck but rather guided to a safer place, informed by self-determination. Reaching this capacity involves the development of new understandings and testing of new actions. A decolonizing approach to embodied theater pedagogy is all about being safe enough to be dangerous. Salverson (1996) reminded us to examine "in what context are risky stories being told? Within what frameworks did they originate? And what is the cost to the speaker?" (p. 181). Linde Zingaro (2009, p. 15) argued that there are always disclosure consequences that need to be assessed before inviting others to tell their stories or telling our own.

In choosing to ask groups to immerse themselves in theatrical processes and theater making, facilitators activate a potent but demanding path. While they can create conditions for immense self-learning, decolonization via assisting to reconnect body and mind, and the honoring of painful and sometimes heroic histories, they can also set off processes that are dangerous to individuals and to groups. Educators and facilitators take on these responsibilities often, and in the interests of enfranchisement, decolonization, and creation of agency, we suggest that the following principles and commitments be adopted.

This work requires a form of *attention*, using all our senses. We walk with others, looking, seeing, listening, and hearing, remaining deeply curious, gathering cues and information along the way. We must *assess the costs, risks, and benefits* as fully as we can, given that much cannot be known for sure. We need to *invent* in response to our community rather than impose a theater process recipe. While we must be cautious, we must also *be willing to move forward*, not blindly but with hearts and eyes wide open, not knowing the future. Embodied theater processes can lead to self-revelation beyond a comfort zone. We should not invite or encourage such disclosures unless they can be fully heard, held, honored, and tapped into for the knowledge within the experience. These stories *are gifts that must be handled with care in gentle yet strong containers*. When we decide to use embodied theater processes, we must *let people know what the process will be* and inform them that that these processes can be powerful and can unleash surprising experiences. We should *explore individual and group self-care capacity* and create conditions that enable safety as we encourage courageous exploration. We need to *ask what agreements we have to move forward*, to try new things. We need to *make the work count*. This work is not about stories being told. It is about the telling and the listening, and engaging with the truth of stories *to inform action*.

References

Asher, N. "At the Interstices: Engaging Postcolonial and Feminist Perspectives for a Multicultural Education Pedagogy in the South." *Teachers College Record*, 2005, *107*(5), 1079–1106.

Butler, J. "Performative Acts and Gender Constitution: An Essay in Phenomenology and Gender Theory." In J. H. Bial (ed.), *The Performance Study Reader*. New York: Routledge, 2004.

Butterwick, S., and Selman, J. "Deep Listening in a Feminist Popular Theatre Project: Upsetting the Position of Audience in Participatory Education." *Adult Education Quarterly*, 2003, 53(4), 7–23.

Freire, P. *Pedagogy of the Oppressed*. New York: Continuum, 1983.

Hurren, W., Moskal, M., and Wasylowich, N. They are Always Watching Me: A Reader's Theatre Script Based on the Performative Aspects of Be(com)ing Teachers. *Teaching Education*, 2001, 12(3), 335–345.

Jackson, A. *Theatre, Education and the Making of Meanings: Art or Instrument?* Manchester, United Kingdom: Manchester University Press, 2007.

Jaggar, A. "Love and Knowledge." In A. Jaggar and S. Bordo (eds.), *Gender/Body/Knowledge—Feminist Reconstructions of Being and Knowing*. New Brunswick, N.J.: Rutgers University Press, 1992.

Joy, P., and Hood, R. J. (producers and directors). *Creating Bridges: Puente Theatre* [Film]. Victoria, British Columbia: National Film Board of Canada, 1988.

Kidd, R. "Liberation or Domestication: Popular Theatre and Non-Formal Education in Africa." *Educational Broadcasting International*, 1979, 12(1): 3–9.

Masschelein, J. "E-ducating the Gaze: The Idea of a Poor Pedagogy." *Ethics and Education*, 2010, 5(1), 43–53.

Mezirow, J. "Transformative Learning: Theory to Practice." In P. Cranton (ed.), *Transformative Learning in Action: Insights from Practice*. New Directions for Adult and Continuing Education, no. 74. San Francisco: Jossey-Bass, 1997.

Nicholson, H. *Applied Drama: The Gift of Theatre*. London, United Kingdom: Palgrave Macmillan, 2005.

Prentki, T., and Selman, J. *Popular Theatre in Political Culture: Britain and Canada in Focus*. Bristol, United Kingdom: Intellect, 2000.

Salverson, J. "Performing Emergency: Witnessing, Popular Theatre, and the Lie of the Literal." *Theatre Topics*, 1996, 6(2), 181–191.

Selman, J. *Role Play: A Practical Guide for Group Leaders*. Edmonton, Canada: AADAC Publications, 1986.

Tejedes, C., and Espinoza, M. "Toward a Decolonizing Pedagogy: Social Justice Reconsidered." In P. P. Trifonas (ed.), *Pedagogies of Difference: Rethinking Education for Social Change*. New York: Routledge, 2003.

Young, I. M. *Justice and the Politics of Difference*. Princeton, N.J.: Princeton University Press, 1990.

Zingaro, L. *Speaking Out: Storytelling for Social Change*. Walnut Creek, Calif.: Left Coast Press, 2009.

SHAUNA BUTTERWICK is associate professor of adult education in the Department of Educational Studies, University of British Columbia.

JAN SELMAN is professor of acting, directing, and community-based theater in the Department of Drama, University of Alberta.

This article synthesizes key ideas from the volume, emphasizing the role of embodied knowing in becoming fully actualized human beings.

Coming Full Circle: Reclaiming the Body

Randee Lipson Lawrence

We come into the world as embodied beings. As infants we quickly become curious about our own bodies, often staring at our hands for hours. As small children we unselfconsciously dance, twirl, and climb. As we age we learn to become embarrassed, often feeling awkward and uncomfortable in our own bodies. When we enter formal education, learning is perceived as something we do in our heads. Yet as the articles in this volume show, the body is also a source of knowledge. Without embodied knowledge, we cannot experience the full range of epistemological possibilities. As Celeste Snowber proclaims in Chapter Six: "Kinesthetic knowing is central to being human. . . . We need our full bodies for deeper understanding of what it means to be human in this world."

This volume has explored embodied knowing in formal and informal education, including the university classroom, the workplace, the health professions, and the community. We considered the role of intuition, theater, dance, yoga, and outdoor education activities as forms of embodied learning. While the contexts of education were different, six major themes emerged as common threads of the articles. These include: body wisdom, the role of the body in holistic learning, the role of the body in increasing awareness of self and others, the body in experiential and transformative learning, body pedagogy, and challenging dominant ideology through decolonization of the body.

Body Wisdom

We hold deep knowledge and wisdom in our bodies. This knowledge is often stored in our unconscious (Jung, 1964). Getting in touch with embodied knowledge involves surfacing knowledge that is often hidden from our awareness. Our body has a memory of its own that holds stories and potential traumatic experiences. We need to learn to listen to our bodies to tap into this wisdom. The articles in this volume discussed multiple ways to "re-present" knowledge through our bodies including movement, dance, drama, and enacting physical challenges.

Surfacing Preconscious Knowledge. In Chapter One I discussed how much of our knowledge is intuitive. This knowledge is present but often hidden from our immediate awareness. To tap into this unconscious knowledge, we need to pay more attention to our bodies. As Ann L. Swartz tells us in Chapter Two, this knowledge comes to us without language. Artistic expression can be a way to get in touch with embodied knowledge (Lawrence, 2008). Snowber (Chapter Six) says, "When we write from our sweat, our words uncover knowing that we did not know." As a dancer, Snowber is truly talking about writing from sweat; however we can also "sweat" out our knowledge through painting, poetry, or song.

Body Memory. The body is a container for stories that each of us hold. Swartz (Chapter Two), Yolanda Nieves (Chapter Four), and Shauna Butterwick and Jan Selman (Chapter Seven) all discuss how these stories can be cultural, political, and sometimes traumatic. Nieves reminds us of the importance of trusting the location of knowledge in our bodies and equates it with cultural awareness. Butterwick and Selman caution that surfacing hidden knowledge may bring up repressed emotions that need to be handled with sensitivity.

Listening to the Body. Pamela Meyer asks in Chapter Three: "What if the body was valued as a site of learning in organizations? What knowledge would become valid?" Valuing body knowledge and wisdom involves deep listening. The body often knows what it needs. Swartz illustrates this well in Chapter Two relative to health care: "My body 'suggested' things it desired and I acted . . . my body instructed me in healing."

Re-Presenting Knowledge through the Body. Paying attention to the body and recovering stories are ways to surface hidden knowledge. We can also use our bodies to share our knowledge or, as Nieves (Chapter Four), says "re-present" our knowledge: "My embodiment of the women's narratives and the writing of the text became an act of thinking with the heart. And my heart, joined with the interviews, demanded poetry, song, and body movement—all ways that a body can re-present knowledge." For Nieves, the only way this knowledge could be adequately expressed was through the body. Similarly, Snowber (Chapter Six) talks about using the body as a place of inquiry to have a deeper engagement with our questions and come to a greater understanding: "By dancing our questions, we can uncover the questions underneath the questions and open up a deep listening to the body's knowledge."

Role of the Body in Holistic Learning

All of the authors agreed that embodied learning is an essential component of a holistic model of learning. It cannot be separated from other forms of learning. Learning encompasses the body, mind, heart, and spirit. Embodied learning requires whole-person engagement. Getting into our bodies can help prevent overthinking an issue, which can lead to inaction. The various articles also made linkages to other forms of learning.

Body, Mind, Heart, and Spirit in Learning. In Chapter One I introduced an intuitive model of learning that began with knowing in the body but made linkages to other ways of knowing, including cognitive, affective, and spiritual knowing. Most of the authors agreed that these ways of learning are inextricably connected. Snowber even goes so far as to say "Dance is needed as we recover what it means to be adults in the world, learning with mind, body, and soul." Cognitive learning, which is privileged in our Western educational system, is indeed only one form of learning and needs these other forms of learning to complete us as human beings.

Whole-Person Engagement. In introducing improvisational games into the workplace, Meyer discovered that through embodied experience, her participants felt safe to bring their whole selves to the learning experience, which she described as transformative for the learners. She called this "whole-body engagement." This is similar to what Yorks and Kasl (2002) referred to as "whole person learning," which occurs out of direct experiential engagement. Affective and imaginal knowing are valued along with the practical. In other words, the learning is holistic.

Pitfalls of Overthinking. The connections among mind, body, and emotion are clearly illustrated by Eric Howden in Chapter Five as he describes his experience with adult learners on an outdoor adventure course. These learners are given a set of physical challenges that seem frightening and almost beyond their ability. Once they realize that they are overthinking the situation—that is, that their minds are giving them messages that stop them from succeeding—they get into their bodies and find that their confidence increases with each small physical success. According to Howden, "There is an undeniable connection between the physical and the mental."

Linkages to Other Forms of Learning. In addition to the relationship of embodied knowing to cognitive, affective, and spiritual ways of knowing, the authors discussed other linkages. Nieves quoted Wilcox (2009, p. 105): "Lived experiences, performance, and bodily intelligence are three interconnected concepts that help us consider and practice embodied ways of knowing in education." Snowber linked embodied knowing to imaginative thinking and kinesthetic intelligence to "visual, tactile, mental, cognitive, and emotional intelligence." Butterwick and Selman connected knowing through the body with intuition and inspiration.

Knowing is clearly a holistic process that cannot be explained by reason alone. Embodied knowing along with reason helps us to understand ourselves more fully as human beings.

Awareness of Self and Others

Many of the authors discussed how engagement in embodied activities results in increased self-awareness. It also increases sensitivity to others, which makes for improved collaborative relationships. Additionally, embodied knowing leads to personal empowerment for some learners.

Self-Awareness. Listening to one's body—that is, really tuning in to what one is feeling, not only physically but emotionally as well—is a discipline. Once one learns to do this, one becomes aware that these sensations are happening all of the time. Swartz, who is a nurse, wrote about health care contexts. She noticed, from her own experience and that of her patients, that we can learn to listen to our bodies and that our bodies would tell us if they were ill and what kinds of attention were needed. Howden discovered that people in outdoor adventure courses often experienced both mental and physical distress but that this distress often opened up "opportunities to break down barriers and open the potential for self-discovery."

Relational Knowledge. Meyer, Howden, and Swartz all talked about relational knowledge and interconnectedness generated through embodied group activities. Having a shared embodied experience can bring groups closer and increase bonds. It creates shared memory, which can enhance communication. Meyer stated that learners "feel more comfortable asking for help because of the bonds they build through these embodied and whole-person experiences. . . . Relational knowledge is embedded in the relationships themselves and is gained through shared experience." Howden wrote how shared experience, especially when dealing with difficult physical challenges, can help to build bonds and strengthen interpersonal relationships. Participants see each other at their weakest and most vulnerable, which often links them in profound ways. Swartz talked about how group reflection of shared experience often leads to collaborative knowledge and group insight.

Personal Empowerment. Growth in confidence about one's ability to act on one's own behalf was another outcome of embodied learning. Howden found that when the level of physical challenge was incrementally increased, participants experienced growth in their levels of confidence. They felt empowered to take on even greater challenges. Swartz talked about the empowerment that happens when one listens to and takes seriously messages from one's own body about health care needs rather than blindly relying on the advice of medical experts: "At the whole-body level, gaining learning confidence in one's ability to read the environment and respond to it effectively supports confidence in one's ability to survive."

Experiential and Transformative Learning

Embodied learning is by nature experiential. You have to do something, even if that something is simply becoming aware of bodily sensations. Because embodied knowing is often a profound physical, emotional, mental, and spiritual experience, it has the potential for transformative learning as well.

Experiential Learning. To *embody* is to physically experience learning through yoga, dance, climbing ropes, improvisation, theater exercises, or any other activity involving the body. As Snowber expressed: "We came from the belly and hips and we must return there. This isn't knowledge that can just be told or read about; it must be experienced." Kolb (1984) developed a four-stage model of experiential learning that includes the actual experience, reflection on the experience, forming new knowledge or understanding, and finally application of the knowledge to new situations. While this model is not as linear as it seems, all of the authors in one way or another talked about these components of learning in relationship to embodiment. For example Howden engaged his learners in group reflection as a way to debrief their physical experience, an activity that offered "great insight into the actions and behaviors of individuals and groups." He offered opportunities to extend this learning by encouraging participants to develop a plan of action for how they could apply what they learned to other aspects of their lives.

Transformative Learning. Several of the authors discussed how embodied learning was transformative for some learners as they experienced a shift in worldview or reported in some way being changed. Meyer referred to this as a "mind-set shift from workplace to playspace" as her participants began to rethink what could happen in their place of work. Butterwick and Selman, and Nieves talked about how theater can be a space for transformation. To quote Nieves: "My entire body engaged in a physical and spiritual shape-shifting." Snowber talked about the movement of dance as an invitation to "reimagine new worlds." Howden emphasized how adventure education offered opportunities to "break through physical and mental barriers" that left people forever changed.

Embodied learning is experiential learning. As Kolb (1984) and others have argued, the learning is not simply in the doing but in making sense of the experience through reflection. As embodied experiences are often deep and meaningful for the learner, they are ripe for transformative learning to occur.

Body Pedagogy

We've talked about learning in a variety of different ways, but how does one teach in an embodied way? In the various articles the authors discussed the role of the educator, facilitating embodied instructional activities, and dealing with learner resistance.

Role of the Educator. As Snowber pointed out, "we teach with and through our bodies." Our bodies convey to students when we are excited about what we are teaching and when we are bored, tired, or engaged. Educators are also models. As Meyer explained, if an instructor comes with a "playful spirit," it can be an invitation for students to play. I talked about the importance of gauging students' level of engagement by observing body cues. Butterwick and Selman elaborated on the importance of the educator creating a safe container where hidden embodied memories that may surface can be dealt with in sensitive ways.

Facilitating Instructional Activities. Embodied teaching can take on many forms. Meyer suggests calling students' attention to their bodies by asking them to take some conscious breaths. She also uses improvisational games and encourages learners to express embodied knowledge through drawing and performance. Snowber advocates "dance as a way of inquiry." By "dancing our questions" or using our whole bodies to inquire, we can move to a deeper level of knowing. Swartz facilitates what she refers to as "clinical action pedagogy": she guides her students in embodied activities like yoga trance dance, drawing of life-size body images, and using their bodies to tell stories. Butterwick and Selman engage students in theater activities to increase awareness of racism, sexism, and homophobia to promote decolonization and provoke social action. I also discussed embodying stories through body movement, dance, or theater activities to tap into knowledge that cannot be expressed verbally.

Learner Resistance. As enlivening and enlightening as embodied pedagogy can be, educators need to acknowledge that this way of teaching goes against the grain of what most learners are used to and comfortable with. We never know where our learners have been and what kinds of baggage they carry. While there are ways to gradually increase student comfort level by starting with the least threatening kinds of activities, no one should be forced to engage. As I suggested and Butterwick and Selman emphasized, any kinds of embodied pedagogy requires a great deal of sensitivity on the part of the educator to protect the safety and privacy of the individual learners.

If adult educators are willing to move outside of the boundaries of traditional higher education pedagogy with its reliance on verbal and textual knowledge, new learning opportunities can emerge.

Challenging Dominant Ideology About the Body

The authors of this volume are in agreement that learning through the body is problematic. Promoting and practicing embodied pedagogy often means breaking through boundaries and challenging dominant ideologies and epistemologies that tell us our minds are the primary sources of learning. We discuss challenging assumptions about the body as well as assumptions about the meaning of work and education. We offer counternarratives to privileging rationality in learning and offer insight on embodied learning as a form of decolonization, making way for the liberation of subjugated knowledge.

Assumptions About the Body. The articles in this volume have shown how embodied learning is a way of challenging hegemonic assumptions that the body is a source of embarrassment and has no place in our educational programs. Nieves referred to the body as a terrain of struggle, meaning that many of our repressed memories of oppression are housed in the body. We naturally live in our bodies as children, but as we age we learn to become embarrassed and ashamed of our bodies. As Snowber said, "It is clear that body knowledge has become endangered within the human species, and we are often alienated in our own bodies." Conscious attention to embodied learning disrupts these notions, allowing us to reclaim the body as a source of knowledge.

Assumptions About Work and Education. The articles also challenge assumptions about the meaning of work as well as education. Meyer talked about how many of us were raised to believe that the workplace was a place for work and not for play. Snowber and I both discussed how formal schooling conditioned us to sit still rather than move around. Even in traditional adult and higher education, we sit in desks for the majority of our learning. As the articles show, learning happens experientially through the body. To allow for this learning to occur, we need to shift our assumptions and explore new spaces and terrains where it is likely to flourish.

Counternarratives to Privileging Rationality. I as well as other authors talked about the limitations of privileging rational thinking as the dominant way of knowing in education. As I said in Chapter One, the overemphasis on rationality "deprives us of fully actualizing ourselves as human beings." I also discussed how feminist discourse can be a way of reclaiming the body's knowledge. To move embodied knowing from the margins to the center of learning in adult education, we need to develop counternarratives that make use of our bodies, our spirit, and our emotions as well as our minds.

Embodied Learning as Decolonization. The dominance of rational ways of learning in education can be a colonizing process, particularly for members of oppressed groups and cultures where other ways of knowing are regularly practiced. As Butterwick and Selman pointed out, colonization separates mind from body, which leaves one open to "domination and manipulation." They see theater as a way of decolonizing by bringing mind and body back together. Nieves talked about theater as a way to reclaim subjugated truths and "free repressed social, cultural, and political history." These truths come through the body, allowing performers as well as audiences to resist colonization. In this way, as Butterwick and Selman state, new knowledge is generated that leads to enfranchisement and action.

Coming Full Circle

This volume has attempted to bring learning back to its roots, when learning through the body was as natural as breathing. As adult educators, we need to understand the many ways adults learn and design learning strategies to meet the needs of an increasingly diverse group of learners. An understanding of how we come to know and learn through the body helps us to imagine new realities, opening us up to greater possibilities for creating more inclusive spaces for our learners.

References

Jung, C. G. (ed.). *Man and His Symbols.* New York: Dell, 1964.
Kolb, D. A. *Experiential Learning.* Englewood Cliffs, N.J.: Prentice-Hall. 1984.
Lawrence, R. L. "Powerful Feelings: Exploring the Affective Domain of Informal and Arts-Based Learning." In J. Dirkx (ed.), *Adult Learning and the Emotional Self.* New Directions for Adult and Continuing Education, no. 120. San Francisco: Jossey-Bass, 2008.
Wilcox, H. N. "Embodied Ways of Knowing, Pedagogies, and Social Justice: Inclusive Science and Beyond." *NWSA Journal,* 2009, *21*(2), 104–120.
Yorks, L., and Kasl, E. "Toward a Theory and Practice for Whole-Person Learning: Reconceptualizing Experience and the Role of Affect." *Adult Education Quarterly,* 2002 52(3),176–192.

RANDEE LIPSON LAWRENCE is an associate professor of adult and continuing education at National Louis University in Chicago.

INDEX

Page references followed by *fig* indicate an illustrated figure.

Aboriginal people: theater used for embodied knowledge of decolonization, 63–65, 77; theater used for witnessing and embodiment of, 65–67
Adult education: challenging assumptions about, 77; implications of embodied knowledge through theater for, 67–68; implications of women's stories for, 41; limitations of privileging rational thinking in, 77; patient education and role of, 18
Amabile, T. M., 26
Anzaldua, G. A., 35
Asher, N., 63

Baker, B., 25–26
Barry, D., 26
Bastable, S., 17
Baumgartner, L., 1
Bell, D., 35
Biodots, 22
Blanchard, M., 5
Bloom, B. S., 6
Bloom taxonomy, 6
Blumenfeld-Jones, D., 54
Bodily-kinesthetic intelligence, 6
Body: assumptions about the, 77; challenging dominant ideology about the, 76–77; as container of memory of stories, 72; learning to listen to our, 72; re-presenting knowledge through the, 72; social resistance role of the, 11. *See also* Embodied learning
"The Body Knows" (poem), 58–59
Body language: embodied pedagogy on becoming aware of, 11; metaphors created to express knowledge of, 9
Body pedagogy: facilitating instructional activities for, 76; learner resistance to, 76; role of the educator in, 76; understanding the, 75
Body wisdom, 71–72
Body-mind connections: dance as way of knowing using, 53–59; description of, 16; outdoor experiential education using, 43–50, 73; theater experienced through, 61–68
Body-subject discourse, 10

Body/somatic knowledge, 6
Boucouvalas, M., 1
Boud, D., 43, 50
Bresler, L., 54
The Brown Girls' Chronicles: Puerto Rican Women and Resilience (Vida Bella Ensemble), 38–41
Butler, J., 62
Butterwick, S., 2, 9, 10, 61, 66, 69, 72, 73, 75, 76, 77

Caffarella, R., 1
Canadian Popular Theatre Alliance Festival, 63–64
Cancienne, M. B., 54, 57
Cartesian dualistic belief: contesting the, 1; feminist discourse rejecting the, 10
Chicago Center for the Performing Arts: *The Brown Girls' Chronicles* performed at, 38–40; outcomes of the performance at, 40–41
"Choreographing resistances," 11
Clark, M. C., 10
Clinical action pedagogy: description of, 19; outcomes of embodied, 22–23; wheel of, 21*fig*
Clinical care: clinical action pedagogy, 19–23; examining how embodied learning can be applied to, 15–16; patient education context of, 17–19
Cognitive knowledge, 7*fig*, 8, 73, 77
Cognitive learning, 73
Collective engagement: embodying through women's stories, 37–38; relational knowledge generated by, 28, 64; social activism through, 11, 33–41, 64
Colonizer/oppressor, 63. *See also* Decolonization
Conscious embodiment, 8
Consciousing, 9
Consciousness: coflating terms of embodiment and, 17; definition of, 8
Counterstorytelling: description of, 36; women's stories framed by CRT and CRF, 35–37
Crabtree, B. F., 19, 20, 21
Creating Bridges (video documentary), 64

79

Critical race feminism (CRF), 35
Critical race theory (CRT), 35–36
Crowdes, M. S., 8

Dagiantis, B., 28–29
Damasio, A. R., 8, 10
Dance: as a birthright, 53–54; embodied knowledge expressed through, 9; functioning as embodied knowing, 54–55; literacy connection to, 56–57; playing as, 55–56; thinking in movement component of, 55; transformative learning through, 73; as way of inquiry, 57–59
Decolonization: embodied learning as, 77; examining the social transformation of, 63; theater used for embodied knowing of, 63–65; witnessing through theater for embodied knowledge of, 65–67. *See also* Colonizer/ oppressor
Delgado, R., 35
Denzin, N. K., 36
Depression, 16
Descartes, R., 1, 10
Dewey, J., 43, 44
Dirkx, J., 1, 6, 8

Education. *See* Adult education
Elkington, J., 27
Embodied activities: dance as, 9, 53–59, 73; facilitating instructional and, 11, 76; Mightybytes' practice of, 27–30; outdoor experiential education using, 43–51, 73; relational knowledge generated through, 28, 64; theater as, 61–68, 77
Embodied awareness, 31. *See also* Self-awareness
Embodied cognition, 17
Embodied knowing: description of, 6; theater's pedagogy to create, 61–68
Embodied knowledge: from conscious engagement with our bodies, 9; examples of getting in touch with, 9–10; feminism scholarship on, 10; imagining a pedagogy of, 10–12; learner resistance to, 11–12, 76
Embodied learning: applied to clinical settings, 15–23; definitions of, 1, 16–17; examined through different perspectives, 1–2; implications for practitioners, 30–31; learner resistance to, 11–12; Mightbytes' embodied practices for, 28–30; other terms that relate to, 6; outdoor experiential education approach to, 43–51, 73; as transformative, 29, 61–68, 75; women's stories for embodied knowing and, 33–41. *See also* Body; Knowing; Somatic learning
Embodied learning benefits: embodied transformative learning, 29; energy and engagement, 28; improved collaboration, 28–29; "it's not like work" theme of, 29; relational knowledge, 28, 74
EMDR (eye movement desensitization and reprocessing), 16
Emotions: consciousing, 9; how telling stories reveals, 9; relationship between motion and, 8
English, L. M., 1
Espinoza, M., 62
Experiential education: avoiding overthinking during, 73; benefits and different approaches to, 75; bringing the physical into learning through, 44; current practices in, 46–47; extension of embodied experience through, 44–45; Helium Hoop activity of, 48–49; high-ropes course, 49–50; as it is currently defined, 45; Kurt Hahn's development of, 45–46; learning through the body using, 43–44; reflective learning from, 50–51; variety of practices of, 47–50. *See also* Transformative learning

Feminism: body-subject discourse in, 10; CRF (critical race feminism), 35
Foucault, M., 66
Fraleigh, S., 57
Freiler, T. J., 6, 11, 16
Freire, P., 20, 66

Gardner, H., 6
Gass, M., 45, 46
Gillen, M. A., 1
Goodman, A., 38
Gradner's multiple intelligences, 6
Graham, M., 54
Guevara, L. de, 64
"Gut feeling," 9, 34

Hahn, K., 45–46, 51
Halprin, A., 57
Hanna, J. L., 56, 57
Hazen, M. A., 26

Heart (affective knowledge), 7fig, 8, 73
Helium Hoop activity, 48–49
High-ropes course, 49–50
Holistic learning: integrated and linked ways of, 6–8, 73; intuitive model of, 6–8, 73; whole-person engagement in, 26–27, 73
Hood, R. J., 64, 65
Horsfall, D., 9, 11
Howden, E., 2, 43, 51, 73, 74
Huerta, Y., 64
Humboldt Park community (Chicago), 37–38
Hurren, W., 61

I Wasn't Born Here: Stories of Latin American Immigrant Women (video documentary), 64
"Implicated audience," 66
Intuition: definition of, 5; expressed as "gut feeling," 9, 34; as type of energy, 34
Intuitive holistic knowing: description of, 6–8, 73; illustrated diagram of, 7fig, 73
Intuitive knowing: description of, 5; sources of, 5–6

Jackson, A., 62
Jagger, A., 67
Jaramillo, N., 2
Jordi, R., 16
Joy, P., 64, 65
Jung, C. G., 5, 71

Kasl, E., 73
Kelso, J.A.S., 17
Kemmis, S., 20
Keogh, R., 43, 50
Kidd, R., 62
Kinesthetic learners, description of, 6
Knowing: dance as way of, 9, 53–59; embodied, 6, 40–41; integrated ways of, 6–8, 73; intuitive, 5–6. *See also* Embodied learning
Knowledge: body wisdom form of, 71–72; body/somatic, 6; conceived as an energy force, 33–34; connecting "I" and group "we," 22; heart (affective knowledge), 7fig, 8, 73; mind (cognitive knowledge), 7fig, 8, 73; re-presented through the body, 72; relational, 28, 74; spiritual domain of, 7fig, 8, 73; surfacing preconscious, 72
Kolb, D., 47, 75

Latino critical race theory (LatCrit), 35
Lawrence, R. L., 2, 3, 5, 6, 8, 9, 10, 13, 24, 71, 72, 78
Learner resistance: to embodied knowledge, 11–12, 76; of feminist discourse to Cartesian dualistic belief, 10
Learning. *See* Embodied learning
Lewis, L., 47

McHose, C., 19
McTaggart, R., 20
Mainemelis, C., 29
Malewski, E., 2, 54
Mason, P. H., 56
Masschelein, J., 66, 67
Meagley, G., 64–65
Megibow, A., 54
Merriam, S., 1
Meyer, P., 1, 2, 25, 26, 29, 30, 32, 72, 73, 74, 75, 76
Mezirow, J., 8, 29, 66
Michelson, E., 10
Mightbytes (Chicago): benefits of embodied learning practices at, 28–30; embodied learning activities at, 27–28
Miller, J. P., 1
Miller, W. L., 19, 20, 21
Mind (cognitive knowledge), 7fig, 8, 73
Miner, J., 46, 51
Moskal, M., 61

Nicholson, H., 64, 66
Nieves, Y., 2, 33, 42, 72, 73, 75
"Now what?" question, 50
Nursing care: clinical action pedagogy approach to, 19–23; examining how embodied learning can be applied to, 15–16; patient education context of, 17–19

Olsen, A., 19
Organizations: embodied learning implications for implementing in, 30–31; Umpaqua Bank's embodied strategies, 25–26; whole-person engagement embraced by, 26–27, 73. *See also* Workplace
Ortega y Gasset, J., 8
Outdoor experiential education. *See* Experiential education

Palmer, P., 55
Park, P., 28
Participatory wheel of inquiry, 19–20
Parviainen, J., 6, 8, 11
Pascale, R. T., 20
Patient education: adult education role in, 18; clinical action pedagogy of, 19–22; development and function of, 17–18; embodied clinical action pedagogy outcomes for, 22–23; re-visioning as embodied learning for health, 18–19
Patient self-caring: clinical action pedagogy on, 19–23; examining how embodied learning can be applied to, 15–16; patient education context of, 17–19
Pedagogy: body, 75–76; clinical action, 19–23; imagining an embodied knowledge, 10–12; theater's, 61–68
Personal empowerment, 74
Pinar, W., 54
Play of dance, 55–56
Playspace: embodied learning to create a, 26; shifting mind-set from workplace to, 30; transformative learning through, 75; workplace benefits of, 32
Popular theater, 62
Porter, P., 54, 57
Positive deviance, 20
Preconscious knowledge, 72
Prentki, T., 62, 63
Priest, S., 45, 46
Privileging rationality, 7fig, 8, 73, 77

Rational thinking, 7fig, 8, 73, 77
Reflection: experiential education encouragement of, 47, 50–51; "Now what?" question for, 50; "So what?" question for, 50; "What?" question for, 50
Relational knowledge, 28, 64
Resistance: of feminist discourse to Cartesian dualistic belief, 10; of learners to embodied knowledge, 11–12, 76; role that the body plays in social, 11
Richards, A., 45, 46
Richmond, S., 54
Ronson, S., 29
Rosch, E., 17

The Safety and Power of Fiction, 66
Salverson, J., 66, 68
Selby, D., 33

Self-awareness: clinical action pedagogy to increase, 19–23; how women's stories promote, 33–41, 64; *I Wasn't Born Here: Stories of Latin American Immigrant Women* (video documentary) promoting, 64. See also Embodied awareness
Self-Reiki, 22
Selman, J., 2, 61, 62, 63, 66, 67, 69, 72, 73, 75, 76, 77
Shapiro, S. (Sherry), 9, 10, 57
Shapiro, S. (Svi), 9, 10
Sheets-Johnstone, M., 55
Shilling, C., 11
Siegel, D. J., 17
Smith, L. B., 17
Snowber, C., 2, 53, 54, 55, 56, 57, 60, 71, 72, 75, 76, 77
"So what?" question, 50
Social activism: *I Wasn't Born Here:* (video documentary) promoting awareness and, 64; role that the body plays in, 11; through women's stories, 33–41, 76
Somatic learning, 6, 16. See also Embodied learning
Spatial intelligence, 6
Spiritual knowledge, 7fig, 8, 73
Spolin, V., 25
Stanage, S. M., 9
Stanage's phenomenological model, 9
Stephancic, J., 35
Sternen, J., 20
Stinson, S., 57
Stories: body as container and memory for, 72; community awareness and social action through women's, 33–41, 64; counterstorytelling concept of, 35–37; embodied knowledge expressed through, 9; emotions revealed through, 9. See also Theater
Stress, Biodots used to self-monitor, 22
Stuckey, H., 6, 8, 9
Swartz, A. L., 1, 15, 19, 22, 24, 72, 74, 76

Tai chi, 16
Tejedes, C., 62
Theater: embodied processes to examine decolonization, 62–65, 77; "implicated audience" of, 66; implications for adult educators, 67–68; mind-body connections through, 61–62; popular, 62; The Safety and Power of Fiction in, 66; witnessing through embodiment experience of, 65–67. See also Stories

Thompson, E., 17
Tichen, A., 9, 11
Tisdell, E. J., 19
Transformative learning: dance experienced as, 9, 53–59, 73; embodied learning as, 29, 75; examining theater's pedagogy for, 61–68; shifting from workplace to playspace for, 26, 30, 32, 75. *See also* Experiential education

Umpaqua Bank: "motivational moment" practiced at, 25; value of embodied strategies of, 25–26
Unconscious body wisdom, 71–72

Varela, F. J., 17
Vaughan, F. E., 5
Vida Bella Ensemble, 38–41

Walker, D., 43, 50
Waylowich, N., 61
"What?" question, 50
Wheel of clinical action pedagogy, 21*fig*
Whole-person engagement, 26–27, 73
Wilber, K., 20
Wilcox, H. N., 39–40, 73

Wildcat, D., 63–64
Wing, A. K., 35
Winton-Henry, C., 54, 57
Women's stories: collective engagement through, 37–38; counterstorytelling framed by CRT and CRF, 35–37; embodied ways of knowing through, 40–41; embodying the performance of, 38–40; embodying the possibilities of, 34–35; *I Wasn't Born Here:* (video documentary), 64; implications for adult educators, 41
Workplace: challenging assumptions about, 77; clinical action pedagogy for embodied care at clinical, 19–23; creating playspace in the, 26, 30, 32, 75; Mightbytes' embodied learning practices in the, 27–30; Umpaqua Bank's embodied strategies for the, 25–26. *See also* Organizations

Yorks, L., 73
Young, I. M., 62

Zera, B., 27–28
Zingaro, L., 68

OTHER TITLES AVAILABLE IN THE NEW DIRECTIONS FOR
ADULT AND CONTINUING EDUCATION SERIES
Susan Imel and Jovita M. Ross-Gordon, COEDITORS-IN-CHIEF

For a complete list of back issues, please visit www.josseybass.com/go/ndace

ACE133 **Expanding the Boundaries of Adult Religious Education: Strategies, Techniques, and Partnerships for the New Millennium**
E. Paulette Isaac
The field of adult religious education is rich with opportunities for study and service. This sourcebook brings needed attention to adult religious education as an important site for program creation, teaching, learning, and adult development. It offers insight into the ways that adult religious education serves adult learners. Numerous examples of adult education within and between religious institutions are presented. From this book, practitioners can glean helpful ideas to enhance practice as well as programs; researchers will find it useful as a basis for additional research regarding religious institutions, adult religious education, and adult learners in general.
ISBN: 978-1-1182-9187-0

ACE132 **Challenging Ableism, Understanding Disability, Including Adults with Disabilities in Workplaces and Learning Spaces**
Tonette S. Rocco
At present, no issue of diversity, privilege, or human rights in the field of adult education has been given less attention than disability. This sourcebook aims to broaden the view of disability from a medical or economic concern to a social justice concern. Disability affects adults across the life span, at work, and while seeking further education—and they are the one minority group every person can join. This sourcebook examines practical, theoretical, and research aspects of disability—including those who question disability classifications—and situates it as a political and social justice concern, technical and pragmatic concern, and personal experience. The authors present the perspectives of individuals with disabilities, service providers, parents, and teachers and offer analyses that range from the personal to the broadly political.
ISBN: 978-1-1182-1866-2

ACE131 **Adult Education and the Pursuit of Wisdom**
Elizabeth J. Tisdell, Ann L. Swartz
Times of change always feel complex, and today's world seems to be changing constantly in more ways than we can track. Adult educators working with adult learners desire deeply to act and speak with wisdom that will offer a sense of truth and stability. Further, as lifelong learners, most of us—educators and learners both—are on a quest for wisdom. Indeed, who among us has never wished for wisdom? Perhaps we wanted to do the right thing for someone in trouble, or save a threatened relationship; perhaps we sought wisdom as understood by the ancients, or wondered how to follow a spiritual path in the light of a great wisdom tradition. Maybe we just wanted to maximize our retirement plan so our family would be cared for when we are gone. Adult education has helped us to become more knowledgeable; perhaps it can also expand our capacity for wisdom.

There is little available consideration of the meaning of wisdom in the field of adult education. This volume explores the possibility of educating for wisdom from multiple perspectives, through the insights of several adult education practitioners who share their own experiences and call upon many bodies of literature. Hopefully, it not only will contribute knowledge about wisdom itself, but also will facilitate wise teaching and learning for and by adults.
ISBN: 978-1-1181-3327-9

ACE130 Adult Education for Health and Wellness
Lilian H. Hill

One task of adulthood is caring for one's health, and, for many, caring for the health of children, a spouse or significant other, or aging parents. Health changes over time in response to wellness activities, aging, or disease. Adult learning is central to people's abilities to cope with changing physical abilities, medical conditions, and the changes in lifestyle and social conditions resulting from them. Chapters in this volume address:

- How adults learn while coping with chronic illness
- Curriculum design for a program for parents with special needs children
- Health education within adult literacy, adult basic education, and English as a Second Language classes
- Ways to address the needs of adults who have low levels of health literacy
- Means of increasing cultural competence among health workers to meet the needs of diverse patients
- Community education performed by trained indigenous community health advisors
- Approaches to help adults evaluate and learn from online information
- The influence of globalism on health
- Ways that health education can be a social justice issue

This diversity of arenas prompts new roles for adult educators. They provide health education alone or in collaboration with health professionals, and they educate health professionals about adults' learning needs, especially individuals who have low levels of health literacy and are from diverse cultural backgrounds. They create meaningful curricula, assist individuals to interpret health information, and influence the design of online information. Other important contributions include training local individuals to serve as community health advisors, helping adults cope with health challenges rooted in increasing globalism, and working for social justice. Finally, adult educators can work with communities to create health-related public policy that contributes to improved quality of life.
ISBN: 978-1-1180-8878-4

ACE129 Meeting Adult Learner Needs Through the Nontraditional Doctoral Degree
James P. Pappas, Jerry Jerman

As the world has grown more complex, so have the learning needs of adults who wish to be professionally and personally equipped for a continually changing global environment. Increasingly, so-called nontraditional students have sought additional educational opportunities and advanced credentials for intellectual growth, career advancement, or both. With demand for this highest level of credential increasing, institutions are rethinking their doctoral

programs, and nontraditional doctoral programs have evolved to accommodate the needs of adult students. These programs combine academic rigor with applied knowledge, scholarship, convenience, and flexibility and come in a variety of formats. The colleges and universities—public and private, nonprofit and for-profit—that respond to this increasing market have discovered both a surprising number of committed students and a new revenue stream. This volume of *New Directions for Adult and Continuing Education* explores the emergence of the nontraditional doctoral degree, the characteristics of the nontraditional doctoral student, faculty concerns, program innovation, and unique programs at four institutions. Both scholars and practitioners will find it an interesting and engaging introduction to the topic.
ISBN: 978-1-1180-2763-9

ACE128   The Struggle for Democracy in Adult Education
Dianne Ramdeholl, Tania Giordani, Thomas Heaney, Wendy Yanow
Adult education in the United States has its roots in democracy. Early in the twentieth century, adult education was often described as a "movement," a spontaneous emergence of study circles, town hall meetings, and learning groups, all engaged in better understanding their world to build a better one democratically. Education in its broadest sense—learning to name the world—was at the center of that movement.

At the same time, and at the opposite end of the spectrum, were those who made the leap from lifelong learning to lifelong schooling. Collapse of the almost-movement was inevitable. Educators in the workplace and in formal institutions of learning sought to shape minds, rather than free them. Consequently, adult education grew up alongside a practice that devalued learning for democratic action and stressed adaptation to the workplace, corporate America, and a consumer economy.

Perhaps nostalgia is a lingering desire to return to a past that never was, but many adult educators, including the authors represented in this volume, have been attempting to reclaim their birthright—a critical but steadfast commitment to building democracy. In this book we build on the historic relationship between adult education and democracy. We examine an adult education practice that not only shapes minds, but also seeks to build communities of collaborative action. We explore best practices in shared and informed decision making within different contexts of adult education—in the community, the classroom, and the university—by focusing on various aspects of our work as adult education practitioners.
ISBN: 978-1-1180-0302-2

ACE127   Adult Education in Cultural Institutions: Aquariums, Libraries, Museums, Parks, and Zoos
Edward W. Taylor, Marilyn McKinley Parrish
On any given week millions of adults around the world can be found gathering in libraries, parks, zoos, arboretums, and museums in person or online. These cultural institutions are seen as repositories of knowledge and collections of a community's cultural or natural heritage. However, they are much more. They are structures that promote cognitive change: commons, places of community outside of home and work, where individuals and groups gather to share and discuss ideas. Cultural institutions may be sites of conflict and contestation where economic and political challenges call into question institutional

purpose and mission, and debates emerge over whose story is told. They can also serve as sites of deliberative democracy that foster social change and reform, where community members can engage with challenging and important societal issues. This volume aims to forge a stronger relationship between adult educators and educators within cultural institutions in an effort to better understand adult learning and teaching within these sites of nonformal education and the role these institutions play in society.
ISBN: 978-0-4709-5208-5

ACE126 **Narrative Perspectives on Adult Education**
Marsha Rossiter, M. Carolyn Clark
This volume presents a variety of perspectives on the role of narrative in adult learning and explores how those perspectives can be translated into practice. Interest in narrative among adult educators has been a continuing strand of our professional dialogue for some time, and it continues to grow as we become increasingly appreciative of the multifaceted views of adult learning that are revealed through the narrative lens. The range of narrative applications, implications, and perspectives in adult education is practically limitless. The perspectives included in this sourcebook, while not an exhaustive review, do convey something of the rich variety and scope a narrative approach offers adult learning.
ISBN: 978-0-4708-7465-3

ACE125 **White Privilege and Racism: Perceptions and Actions**
Carole L. Lund, Scipio A. J. Colin, III
White privilege is viewed by many as a birthright and is in essence an existentialist norm that is based upon the power and privilege of pigmentation. Because it is the norm for the white race, this privilege is virtually invisible, but its racist byproducts are not. It becomes common for whites to believe falsely that their privilege was earned by hard work and intellectual superiority; it becomes the center of their worldview. The reality is that when they defend their pigmentary privilege, what they are really saying is that peoples of color have earned their disadvantage. Unless whites recognize this privilege and the consequent racist attitudes and behaviors, they will continue to perpetuate racism in both their personal and professional lives. It is their responsibility to commit to a significant paradigm shift by recognizing their privilege, critiquing the impact on peoples of color, and making the decision to reconfigure their attitudes and alter their behaviors. This volume focuses on facilitating our understanding of the conceptual correlation between white privilege and racism and how these intertwined threads are manifested in selected areas of adult and continuing education practice. Although there seems to be a consensus that this practice reflects sociocultural and intellectual racism, there has been no discussion of linkages between the white racist ideology, white privilege, and white attitudes and behaviors behind that racism.
ISBN: 978-0-4706-3162-1

ACE124 **Reaching Out Across the Border: Canadian Perspectives in Adult Education**
Patricia Cranton, Leona M. English
This volume brings together Canadian scholars and practitioners to articulate a variety of historical, geographical, and political positions

on the field of adult education in Canada. The chapter authors examine the country's interests and discourses and detail Canada's history, educational initiatives, movements, and linguistic struggles. Specifically, the authors address the uniqueness of Canada's emphasis on linking health and adult literacy; the use of video and dialogue to promote adult and literacy education in the North; the historical adult education initiatives such as Frontier College and the Antigonish movement; the special language and cultural issues that define Quebec's role of adult education and training; the development of critical adult education discourse in Canada; the emphasis on environmental adult education; the uniqueness of the community college system; and initiatives in adult education for community development. By describing Canadian accomplishments and lessons learned in adult education, this volume will help inform the practice, research, and studies of adult educators in the United States.
ISBN: 978-0-4705-9259-5

ACE123 **Negotiating Ethical Practice in Adult Education**
Elizabeth J. Burge
Here is a collection for twenty-first-century challenges! One practical philosopher and seven experienced adult educators dig into their driving values, the existing literature, and frank narratives of direct experience to illuminate key lessons in being one's own applied ethicist. In explaining their decision-making and confronting their unease and doubts, the authors emerge as self-aware, context-aware, principled practitioners. But they are not immune to the problems encountered in the intellectual and interpersonal complexities of ethical analysis.

Acknowledging the challenges in moving beyond such reductionist analyses as "right versus wrong," the authors look for negotiated possibilities of "rightness." Negotiation, reflection, and power emerge as three key themes of the reflective chapters. As a reader, you might consider the various thinking strategies offered, in particular the strategy of "sinning bravely." Additional critical thinking about conflicts that hide in the background of our work ought to help unearth some hegemonic uses of concepts such as fairness and justice.

Feel encouraged, feel strong, feel connected as you compare your own issues and thinking with the authors' experience and guidance. The reading journey of this issue of *New Directions for Adult and Continuing Education* will bring you closer to possibilities for more good work in the tough conditions of twenty-first-century adult education.
ISBN: 978-0-4705-3971-2

ACE122 **Social Capital and Women's Support Systems: Networking, Learning, and Surviving**
Carmela R. Nanton, Mary V. Alfred
The concept of social capital goes back to the early twentieth century. Although it has sociological underpinnings, it has been primarily applied in the business arena. Increasingly, over the last two decades, there has been a proliferation of literature that proposes a broader application of the social capital concepts to individuals, communities, societies, and even adult learning.

This monograph applies social capital concepts to women as adult learners in learning communities, as users of technology, and as workers, and then integrates it from the perspective of adult education. We make the case that, because women tend to be more relational than

men, their lives as students are integrally related to the social networks of which they are a part. We recognize that there are certain risks inherent in social capital networks and that gender bias can lead to exclusionary challenges that marginalize women as a group. On that basis, some feminist theorists have suggested that we simply eliminate the idea of social capital because of the inherent bias in the theory's underlying concepts and assumptions. Instead, we propose an integrationist approach that recognizes the relational nature of women, their historical and contemporary use of social capital networks, and the way they leverage such relationships for personal and community transformation.
ISBN: 978-0-4705-3734-3

ACE 121 **Bringing Community to the Adult ESL Classroom**
Clarena Larrotta, Ann K. Brooks
Using the concept of community building as a framework, this volume summarizes and updates readers on the state of adult English as a second language (ESL) education in the United States. It provides a complete description of this population of learners and their learning needs. The various chapters discuss possibilities for community building in the adult ESL classroom, combining research, theory, and practice. Community building is not a new topic; we often discuss it informally with our colleagues and students. However, scant written material exists—with a focus on adult ESL—documenting how it happens or reconciling theory with practitioners' experiences. In this volume, several practitioners and researchers explain the ways in which they use community-building principles in adult ESL settings. The authors' descriptions of applications of community-building principles can help other adult educators implement these ideas in their teaching practice. Our goal is to encourage readers to spark conversation and continuous learning among all who work in this field.
ISBN: 978-0-4704-7955-1

ACE120 **Adult Learning and the Emotional Self**
John M. Dirkx
Emotion is a pervasive force in adult learning—from fear, anxiety, dread, shame, and doubt to hope, excitement, joy, desire, and pride. For the most part, however, practitioners and scholars view the adult learning process as conceptual, rational, and cognitive. If emotion is considered positively, it is as a helpful adjunct to the learning process. More often, it is regarded as a potential barrier that has to be worked through if effective learning is to occur. Although we are only beginning to attend to the powerful role that emotion can play in our lives as teachers and adult learners, a small but growing body of interdisciplinary scholarship provides an opportunity to revisit our earlier assumptions. This volume seeks to build on this emerging scholarship by focusing on the emotional self across a range of adult learning settings: basic and higher education, workplace learning, and formal and informal contexts. The chapters demonstrate, in different ways, the growing integration of emotion into more holistic, constructive ways of learning and knowing. As we attune to the emotional atmosphere in which we work, we stand a better chance of helping adult students achieve their educational goals—and we become better educators in the process.
ISBN: 978-0-4704-4674-4

NEW DIRECTIONS FOR ADULT AND CONTINUING EDUCATION
ORDER FORM SUBSCRIPTION AND SINGLE ISSUES

DISCOUNTED BACK ISSUES:

Use this form to receive 20% off all back issues of *New Directions for Adult and Continuing Education*. All single issues priced at **$23.20** (normally $29.00)

TITLE	ISSUE NO.	ISBN
_____	_____	_____
_____	_____	_____

Call 888-378-2537 or see mailing instructions below. When calling, mention the promotional code JBNND to receive your discount. For a complete list of issues, please visit www.josseybass.com/go/ndace

SUBSCRIPTIONS: (1 YEAR, 4 ISSUES)

☐ New Order   ☐ Renewal

U.S.	☐ Individual: $89	☐ Institutional: $275
CANADA/MEXICO	☐ Individual: $89	☐ Institutional: $315
ALL OTHERS	☐ Individual: $113	☐ Institutional: $349

Call 888-378-2537 or see mailing and pricing instructions below.
Online subscriptions are available at www.onlinelibrary.wiley.com

ORDER TOTALS:

Issue / Subscription Amount: $ _____

Shipping Amount: $ _____
(for single issues only – subscription prices include shipping)

Total Amount: $ _____

SHIPPING CHARGES:
First Item $6.00
Each Add'l Item $2.00

(No sales tax for U.S. subscriptions. Canadian residents, add GST for subscription orders. Individual rate subscriptions must be paid by personal check or credit card. Individual rate subscriptions may not be resold as library copies.)

BILLING & SHIPPING INFORMATION:

☐ **PAYMENT ENCLOSED:** *(U.S. check or money order only. All payments must be in U.S. dollars.)*

☐ **CREDIT CARD:**   ☐ VISA   ☐ MC   ☐ AMEX

Card number _____ Exp. Date _____

Card Holder Name _____ Card Issue # _____

Signature _____ Day Phone _____

☐ **BILL ME:** *(U.S. institutional orders only. Purchase order required.)*

Purchase order # _____
Federal Tax ID 13559302 • GST 89102-8052

Name _____

Address _____

Phone _____ E-mail _____

Copy or detach page and send to: **John Wiley & Sons, One Montgomery Street, Suite 1200, San Francisco, CA 94104-4594**

Order Form can also be faxed to: **888-481-2665**

PROMO JBNND

CPSIA information can be obtained
at www.ICGtesting.com
Printed in the USA
LVHW03s1624050918
589229LV00016B/1218/P
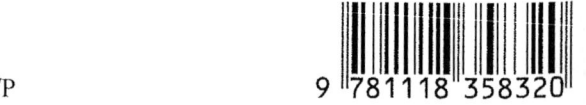